THAT WON'T DO *YOU* ANY GOOD

Humor

Leonard Stegmann

Copyright © by Leonard Stegmann

All rights reserved

Including the right of reproduction

In whole or in part in any form.

ISBN-13: 978-1515158400

ISBN-10: 1515158403

Life has no meaning. You're living in a random universe, and you're leading a meaningless life and everything you've created in your life is going to vanish. —
Woody Allen

TABLE OF CONTENTS

INTRODUCTION 7
Not Without My Hairdryer! 8
The Great Cat Treat Experiment 12
Two Naked Old Men Arguing in a Hot Tub 17
Chocolate Bunnies 20
Ashes to Asses 25
Waldy 29
Clutch Performance 32
A Fish Story 38
An Immodest Proposal 42
You Won't See Me 46
A Dead-On Analogy For Sexagenarians 48
The Watch in the Back of the Drawer 51
Campbell's "Pork" & Beans 56
Weight Loss Scam 59
Brownies 62
How Much Is That Dollar in the Window? 65
An Acre of Sand 69
It'll Be Just Like Starting Over 72
M&M Dreams 75
Nixon Resigns 78
Oh-Fer-Four 81

Herman's Deli	84
Getting a Needle	88
You Bed Your Life	91
With Five Popular Settings	94
I Married a Hoarder	97
File Sharing: 1971 Style	101
No One Will Be Watching Us	103
Cigs	106
Five Whole Dollars	109
At the Military Museum	111
Grandpa Leonard Does It Again	115
Eighteen Cents	118
Mellow Yellow	120
Unconsumed Ice Cream, and Other Myths	122
The Garage Door and the Toilet Seat	126
Kick the Can	131
I Found a Dollar	134
I Could Care Less	137
La Propina	140
Where Am I?	142
Mid-Island Memories	147
The Snack Whore	151
Pillow Talk	153
Spike's New Uncle	156
My Short Career at Short	158

The Snow Shovel 162
Undefeated 166
They Call Me Arroz Con Pollo 168
Putting the Lights on the Christmas Tree 171
T.P. 176
Tapa the Food Chain 179
The China Syndrome 184
The All-Star Game Is Tonight 188
That Bitch! 191
That White Piece of Paper 194
Peter Pan 197
Opposite Day 200
Roger and Me 203
Mom on a Horse 207

INTRODUCTION

❧❧❧❧❧

I was on the telephone telling Mom about the book I had just purchased for a buck at a local garage sale. It was a book of humor, and was nearly one hundred years old. I was, admittedly, a bit awed by the power of books, and that I could be laughing today at something that was written so long ago.

"Just think, Mom," I marveled, "one day somebody could find a copy of one of *my* books in a dusty old garage, and read what I write today a hundred years from now!"

"That won't do *you* any good," said Mom.

And so, if by some miracle you actually *are* reading this book one hundred years from now, well, I certainly hope you enjoy it. Oh, and Mom was right, wasn't she?

That Won't Do You Any Good

Not Without My Hairdryer!

Allow me to begin by admitting that I don't recall being in the best of moods on that long ago day. I may have been grumpy, withdrawn and perhaps even a teensy bit snotty. Still, I didn't believe then, nor do I believe now, that my slightly foul mood was any justification for what she did.

It was about halfway through my traditional weekend visit with my girlfriend, who lived about a half-hour away, and we were taking a walk in a park. I no longer remember the topic of conversation, but something I said had apparently pissed her off. Or, more likely, it was simply a reaction to my overall mood and attitude, as I mentioned above.

What I *do* remember is when we got to her car she opened the driver-side door and slid in, as usual. Her exact words as she did so are gone now, but I remember they included something about teaching me a lesson. And then, rather than unlocking the passenger door to let me in, as I and any other rational human might expect, she simply drove away.

At first I was too dumbfounded to be angry. I waited on the sidewalk for about two minutes, assuming she'd come back and we'd have a good laugh. Well, if not a laugh then at least a heated discussion. But she didn't come back. I had been ditched.

Now, I'm not going to act like she had abandoned me in the heart of some crime-riddled American city or on a wild African savannah where voracious animals prowled. No, the sidewalk I stood numbly on was located in a fairly upscale suburban neighborhood, and it was the middle of the afternoon on a bright, sunny Saturday. But still.

And so I began the not particularly long walk back to my girlfriend's house. Normally it would have been less than a mile to get there, but I had already decided to avoid the direct route and instead travel via some of the winding and fairly unknown back streets. I wasn't sure if my girlfriend had doubled-back to look for me, but I knew at this point the last thing I wanted was for her to find me.

You see, I might have been more surprised than angry when she first pulled away from the curb, but the combination of walking and time had allowed my emotions to percolate a bit, and so by the time I made it back to her home and walked through the front door I was absolutely furious. My plan was, rather than spend the night as I usually would, to gather my things and head directly back home. And she knew it.

Without saying a word I put the few articles of clothing I had brought into my pack and then stalked into the bathroom. It took me about two minutes of frantically looking around before I realized what had happened. My girlfriend had hidden my hairdryer. And damn her if she didn't believe, without a doubt, that I wouldn't go home without it. And she was right.

After refusing to tell me where the hairdryer was, we eventually (well, *I* eventually) calmed down. We talked for a bit and then watched some TV. I ended up staying that night, and we made love as usual. The following day we went out to breakfast, also as usual, and then we said good-bye until the next weekend and I left. And yes, she had finally returned my hairdryer.

I still believe that leaving a lover or friend and driving away, no matter where you are, is a brutal betrayal, something I myself would never do, and most likely never forgive. You might well agree, and if you do you're now wrestling with the concept that I didn't storm out of that house, filled with self-righteous indignation, simply because I didn't have my hairdryer. Well, you're not alone. I'm having trouble believing it myself.

Oh, I could come up with a variety of more rational reasons why I stayed. You want psychological? Okay, maybe deep inside I really wanted to be there, and so was just using the missing hairdryer as an excuse. Or maybe physical? Perhaps I stayed only because I wanted to get laid. Sadly, there is little-to-no truth in either of these explanations.

That hairdryer was as important to me as this story would indicate. I would be going to work on Monday and the hairdryer would be crucial. It wasn't just a matter of not wanting to have wet hair when I left my house. No, it was about the very nature of that hair. My curly locks not only needed to be dried, but to be wrestled with, tamed and styled before going out in public. Otherwise, experience had taught me that I'd look like the aftermath of an explosion in a mattress factory.

"Why didn't you just go and buy another hairdryer?" asked my wife when I told her the story this evening. I suppose I could plead extreme cheapness, but in my defense I'm not sure that back then hairdryers were the inexpensive, throw-away appliances that they are today. And even though I don't recall how much money I made at the time, I assure you it wasn't much. It never has been.

Plus, make no mistake, my natural stubbornness certainly factored into it. I sure as hell was not going to waste money on a *new* hairdryer. After all, I already owned a perfectly usable one, *which that bitch had hidden somewhere in her house!*

What makes me cringe the most when I look back on this incident was that she knew. She could have cried, begged and threatened in order to get me to stay that night, and we both understood it would have been in vain. And yet by simply hiding that hairdryer she had me and she knew it. Check and mate, game over. And it still makes me a little queasy when I think about it.

Leonard Stegmann

The Great Cat Treat Experiment

We've been down this road before. Regular readers (Or am I being delusional again?) will recall the night I drank some absinthe for the first time, and reported the results to you, as it was happening. A few months later I decided to eat some Brussels sprouts for the first time in nearly half a century, and again, you were there. This time I promise you that what I have planned for tonight makes those other adventures pale in comparison.

During those last two experiments I claimed that I was doing what I was doing for one reason alone: for you. I do it all for you, is my frequent mantra. And I do, but this time it's a little different. Tonight's little journey into the unknown has its roots firmly planted in, not my desire to serve you, dear readers, but in my own curiosity. Let me explain:

I arrived home the other night to find Louie waiting for me at the front door. Around back stood Murphy and Opie. Now these may sound like the names of some common thugs (well, maybe not Opie) but they are nothing more than neighborhood cats. At one point or another each of these cats wouldn't come anywhere near me, but over time our relationships have progressed so that I can now pick up any of these cats as if they were lonely orphans and I was a potential adoptive parent.

Why? Because I give out cat treats. Just a crinkle of the foil bag will bring every cat with hearing distance scampering to my home. And some time, as I've already mentioned, they'll be there waiting for me, crinkle or no crinkle. And by the way, my own cat Celine is no better. I've seen her so frantic to be let outside that it seemed as if she would explode if I didn't slide open that door *right now*. And yet all I have to do is shake the treat bag and she turns and looks up at me with those greedy snack eyes. Outside, and everything else not contained in that crinkly bag has, for Celine, ceased to exist.

They're snack whores, every last one of them. And I don't get it. Each day I put out a bowl of dry cat food for Celine. Sometimes it sits there for half a day before she deigns to eat any. And yet if I place a few dry cat treats on the floor, brown morsels that look not much different from the food already in the bowl, I am in danger of being knocked on my ass by a nine pound cat in her manic rush to get to them. Can these two feline edibles really be so different? Is the difference comparable to, say, a bowl of peas and a box of See's candy to we humans?

And so tonight I'm going to take some drastic action; something that would have been totally unimaginable to me just forty-eight hours ago, before I came up with this stupid fucking idea. Yes, in a very short while I am going to eat two tiny bits of crunchy cat food and follow that up with one cat treat. (Incidentally, the treat I'll be consuming is the only kind we buy around here. They're called Temptations, and after all this the least the people who make them could do is to send me a free case or two.)

You know, I think I've run out of things to say, and so, like the preacher who has ended his prayer at an execution, it's time to do what we've all gathered here for. And so now I am going to leave you for a bit, eat some cat food, and then eat one of the cat treats. (Temptations! Buy 'em today!) Oh, and the tasting of the two foods with be separated by a palate-cleansing sip of wine. Or, more likely, a gulp or more. I'll be right back.

Believe it or not, my first reaction to the cat food was a pleasant one. During the first few seconds while I was chewing I was reminded of Cheerios. Then some seasoning kicked in and the stuff in my mouth began to taste *better* than Cheerios. I am not making this up: For a moment or two I seriously thought that this might not be a bad snack to munch while I was watching TV.

The taste reminded me of something, some savory snack that I enjoy, but I couldn't quite place it. I probably could figure it out if I ate a little bit more, but I can tell you right now that won't be happening. You see, after the initial Cheerio taste, after the unidentifiable savory snack taste, came the not overwhelming but certainly not pleasing fish taste. I like fish, when it's served in a restaurant, on a plate with a velvety cream sauce and a side of asparagus. This taste however, was more indicative of a fish that had been discovered after it had rotted in a Dumpster for a few days.

The treat had a very similar taste and feel. It was, perhaps, a little softer and less crunchy, and it again reminded me of something I might be eating out of a box while drinking a beer and watching a football game. Chex Mix? What the treat didn't have was that strong fishy taste.

Still, any notion that I had of these treats tasting like M&M's or even salted cashews is out the window. And I still don't get why the cats go crazy over one more than the other. Could it simply be in the presentation? If so, could cats be conditioned so that if I filled a bowl with the treats they'd let it sit there all day, but would come running when I crinkle a bag now containing only their regular food?

It's possible, I suppose, especially when you take note that cats have a brain the size of a bean. Regardless, I'll save that experiment for another day. I think it's time for me to down another glass of wine. And to brush my teeth. Twice.

Two Naked Old Men Arguing in a Hot Tub

I bet you've never seen two naked old men having an argument in a hot tub. Well, up until a few weeks ago neither had I. I was enjoying the warm, sometimes invasive bubbles of the Jacuzzi at a nudist community in Florida. With me in the hot tub was an old man. We didn't speak, both of us content to experience the soothing effects of the water, each keeping to our own corner of the tub, if a hot tub had corners. Which it doesn't.

I opened my eyes just in time to see another old man gripping the handrail and easing his way down the cement steps and into the hot tub. He was barely in waist-deep when the first old man spoke to him.

"You're supposed to take a shower before you get in," he said.

Which was true. The sign posted on the wall clearly said so. And it's not like it was asking something impossible, since there were three showers not more than five feet from the hot tub steps.

"What?" answered the second old man, doing so in a tone of voice that told me he knew perfectly well what the first old man had said. Nevertheless, the first old man repeated himself.

"You're supposed to take a *shower* before you get into the hot tub," he said, emphasizing his point by indicating the sign on the wall. That's all it took for the first man to explode.

"I took a shower before I left the house and I just took *another* shower by the pool!" he yelled. "How many damn showers am I supposed to take in one day?"

Nudist communities often pride themselves on being peaceful, accepting places where seldom is heard a discouraging word, so this aggressive outburst no doubt caught the first old man off guard.

"C-c-calm down," he stammered. "It's just that we're living in a community here, to keep it nice we —."

"I know it's a community, I live here! Did *you* take a shower before you got in? Good. Then mind your own business!"

And that was all the two naked old men said to each other. As I sat there, my tranquility having been abruptly disturbed, I thought about the argument, and specifically about which of the naked old men I agreed with.

To be sure, the second old man had been rather nasty, when he could have simply said that yes, he had indeed taken a shower. And yet I found myself siding with him. For although the first old man had been correct, and that everyone should shower before getting into the tub, we all at one point or another grow weary of the self-appointed cops who feel it is their solemn duty to make sure that everyone is following the rules.

It brought me back to a time as a child, when I was standing in line at church, waiting to receive Communion. I must have been looking around a bit, when I heard a harsh whisper from the woman standing in line behind me.

"Look straight ahead!" she commanded. Which I immediately did, of course, being much too young and polite to tell this self-righteous old biddy to mind her own goddamn business. I've always thought it would have been wonderful if I had, though.

And so now with the argument ended, the two naked old men (three, if you count me) returned to the business of relaxation. We each closed our eyes and eased back into our own corner of the hot tub, if a hot tub had corners. Which it doesn't.

Leonard Stegmann

Chocolate Bunnies

I'll get two Buddies and a Sweetie, I thought to myself. Excellent. I had been invited that evening to a friend's house for dinner, and having already purchased the requisite bottle of wine, I wanted to pick up something for her three children as well. And as it was just a week before Easter I figured chocolate rabbits would be perfect. The two boys would each get a Buddy Bunny, and the girl a Sweetie Bunny.

I grabbed three of the bunnies off the shelf and headed for the checkout. The plan was working out fine, as both the Buddy Bunny and the Sweetie Bunny weighed fourteen ounces. I knew it wouldn't at all do to give unequal amounts of chocolate to each of the children. Or have kids perhaps changed since I was growing up? I still remember my mother showing me the scrap of paper where she had totaled the prices of the Christmas presents she had bought for my brother and me. The totals were within a few cents of each other. My brother and I were, incidentally, in our thirties at the time. (If I remember correctly, and I do, Mom had spent exactly twenty-eight cents more on my brother than on me. I figure with just a few more years of therapy I'll be over it.)

I was accepting my change from the check-out girl when I noticed it. Somehow I had picked up only one Buddy Bunny and *two* Sweetie Bunnies! Sure, maybe kids have changed, but I doubt so much that a young boy still isn't going to cringe in embarrassment, or scream in outrage, if he gets handed a bunny named Sweetie. Especially if his brother does not.

I explained the situation to the check-out girl and she said, yes, it would be fine if I went back and swapped out the Sweetie for another Buddy. Actually, I don't think she had a clue as to what I was babbling about, and didn't much care. She was, I suspect, due for her break.

When I got back to the chocolate bunny section I was horrified to find that there were no more Buddy Bunnies! Well, that's the way the chocolate crumbles, kids. One of the boys would have to live with the shame that he had received a Sweetie Bunny. I mean, what was he going to do, turn down what was nearly a full pound of free chocolate? I'm sure.

Better yet, what if I gave each of the *boys* a Sweetie and gave the girl the Buddy? Yeah, that's the ticket. After all, it's the 21st century. Let's break down those outdated gender stereotypes! I was still congratulating myself on my Solomon-like solution when I looked down at the plastic bags on the car floor. Was it my imagination or were there only two chocolate bunnies there? I pulled over and frantically opened the plastic bag. What the hell happened to the other Sweetie? (In truth there *was* a third bunny in the bag, a much smaller one that I had also purchased. It was, of course, for me, and doesn't figure prominently in our story.)

It's a bitch and a half to get in and out of the parking lot where I bought the bunnies. I also knew that if I returned to that grocery store and asked that check-out girl if she remembered if I had left a chocolate bunny there, I'd be as familiar to her as an alien that had just beamed down from the Andromeda Galaxy. Probably less so.

Ah, but my brain was still firing on all synapses. I would not let this chocolate bunny fiasco beat me. And so I continued on to the nearby CVS, where I knew they had a fine selection of chocolate bunnies. If luck was with me, and I saw no reason why it would be, they might even have another Buddy Bunny. Now, wouldn't that just solve everything!

They didn't have a Buddy Bunny, of course, but just as I remembered they did have a pretty good assortment. And then I saw him: a not particularly creatively named bunny with the moniker of Peter Rabbit. He looked to be about the same size as Buddy and Sweetie, and so I zoomed in for a closer look. Peter was 13 ounces, just an ounce short of Buddy and Sweetie's fighting weight. Close enough, I thought. If those kids want to quibble over a single ounce of chocolate, have at it. I'm washing my hands of the whole sticky affair.

Not so quickly, though. While I was checking out Peter Rabbit's weight I also noticed more of the description. Goddammit! Peter Rabbit, it seems, was "chocolate-y." It took me several years to train my wife in this regard. Don't buy me a rabbit that's described as "chocolate-y" or "chocolate-flavored" I would instruct her. That means it's not real milk chocolate. And though you'll agree that I am a hypocrite when it comes to many, many things, chocolate is not one of them. I knew then and there that I was not going hand some poor kid a low-rent bunny that was not only an ounce lighter than the rabbits received by his siblings, but was fake chocolate besides. And back onto the shelf hopped that ersatz chocolate rabbit named Peter.

It was then that a rabbit called Bunny Big Ears caught my eye. He's been around a few years now, and is probably the cutest of all the massed produced chocolate bunnies, what with those giant ears and all. And yes, he is indeed chocolate, the real deal. Still, one look and I could tell he didn't weigh nearly as much as Buddy and Sweetie, despite his outsized auricles. A close examination of the box verified that Bunny Big Ears, notwithstanding his grandiose demeanor, weighed but ten ounces.

It is said that the greatest ideas, the best songs, the noblest inventions, often come right out of the blue, suddenly and dramatically, like a bolt of lightning. And that's what happened to me on that day one week before Easter at the CVS store. I picked up Bunny Big Ears, and then also snatched a lesser bunny, one that was so small that he wasn't even given a name by his manufacturer. No matter, because what that bunny *did* have was a description on his much smaller box, and that description told me he weighed exactly…four ounces. And so when combined with Bunny Big Ears' *ten* ounces, well, you get the picture.

And so I arrived at the dinner with my not inexpensive (although certainly by no means expensive) bottle of wine, as well as the chocolate bunnies for the children. I gave Buddy Bunny to one boy, Sweetie Bunny to the girl and Bunny Big Ears and his diminutive and nameless companion to the other boy, each child receiving exactly fourteen ounces of chocolate. And even then, hours after I had come up with this extraordinarily wise solution to the bunny dilemma, I was still basking in the warm glow of my undeniable brilliance. And then I heard it:

"Hey!" said the girl in an indignant voice. "How come he gets *two*?"

Ashes to Asses

"Do you ever go swimming in it?" I asked, gesturing to the beautiful lake in the distance.

"Nah. Too many people's ashes are in there," answered my brother.

It was just about two years after that conversation that I returned to the lake, this time to scatter my brother's ashes. This wasn't any ordinary lake, though, seeing how it was located smack dab in the middle of a popular nudist retreat. This, then, had been my brother's home for the last several years, and having his ashes scattered in that lake had been his request. It was a horrific and tragic time, to be sure, but not without its touches of humor.

Over the years my brother had repeatedly invited my parents to come and visit him in his nudist paradise, and they, not surprisingly, had always declined. Mom, especially, was dead set against the idea, perhaps conjuring in her mind a place running wild with bacchanalian heathens, and naked ones at that. Dad, for his part, was a little more open to visiting, and admittedly curious, but Mom let him know that it was not going to happen. Ever.

And now, with one sentence sloppily written with a cheap ballpoint, my brother had made the impossible a reality. And whether he had intended it as such or not, it was a wonderful final joke. I had offered to go there by myself and scatter the ashes, but my parents wouldn't hear of it. They felt, of course, that they should be there. And so they were.

I notified the community's management of what we were planning to do, and got their permission. By now this sort of thing, as my brother had mentioned, was almost old hat to them. They even offered us the use of an old boat so we could row out to the middle of the lake and do the job right. Mom didn't want to go out in the boat. She didn't say why, and to this day I don't know her reason, but this was not the time for arguing.

And so the four of us, Mom, Dad, Spike and myself, stood along the wooden plank at the edge of the lake. Over my right shoulder the sound of splashing and people laughing threatened to destroy the solemnity of our family ritual. The pool was less than twenty feet away, surrounded by a canvas-covered chain link fence. I couldn't see much of what was going on inside, but I didn't have to. I knew it was a bunch of people, naked people, happily enjoying the gift of another sun-filled day.

I'm sure I said some appropriate words, but I no longer remember what they might have been. I then reached out as far as I could and with a wave of my arm I attempted to scatter my brother's ashes. Instead, the ashes came out of the box in a lump, which plopped down unceremoniously in about three inches of water. I later realized that I should have walked out a few feet into the lake, but I didn't think of it at the time. After all, I'd never done this before.

After a moment everybody headed back to the car. I stayed for another few seconds with my thoughts, and then joined them. Back in the car, Mom admitted that the place really wasn't so bad. I can't say for sure what she had imagined, but the community had a resort atmosphere, with tennis courts, pool, sauna, restaurant, hiking trails and, of course, a lake. The deed, however, was done and so it was clearly time to go. But before we left I did something very nice for my dad.

"Want to take a tour?" I asked him, and he not surprisingly agreed. I offered to let Mom out if she didn't want to go, telling her we'd pick her up in a few minutes, but she declined. And so we slowly drove along the narrow roads to the tents, trailers and small cabins that made up this naked city in the sun.

My intention, of course, was to drive past some naked women for my dad to see. He'd never mention it, and neither would I, but I knew he was curious. Besides, we were already here and it was the least I could do. He'd had a rough day, and it wasn't about to get any easier in the weeks ahead.

It was a quiet day and most of the people must have been at the pool. We had driven through much of the place when we saw her. Dad was finally getting to see a naked woman. Now, this woman was clearly in her late fifties, or even early sixties, but as Dad was at the time pushing eighty, he probably thought he was looking at some naked, young chick. And after all, from his point of view, he was. We drove past her slowly, like the gawkers that we were.

Mission accomplished, I then turned the car around, proceeded slowly to the exit, waved to the people at the gate and headed home. Nobody said much on that hour-long drive. It had been an unusual day, and we each had a lot to think about.

That Won't Do You Any Good

Waldy

ঔ৾ঔ৾ঔ৾ঔ৾ঔ৾

Waldy rode all the way across the country with me last month, and has now found a place in his new, although temporary, home. He stands on the floor in my living room, about six inches from the wall. There's no saying how long Waldy will be with me, so I've decided it's best to simply enjoy him while I can.

Waldy is a ceramic dachshund. He is about a foot and a half long and stands perhaps six inches tall from the floor to the top of his head. He was a gift that my mother gave to my dad's mother many years ago, although the exact details have been lost in the fog of time. As I understand it, Mom bought Waldy for Grandma while she was going out with my dad, but before they got married.

This would make Waldy's purchase date sometime in the late 1940's. My dad had actually had a dachshund, a *real* one, named Waldy as a child, but whether this had been my mother's motivation for buying the ceramic dog I'll never know. It's also possible that she chose it because dachshunds, at the time, were the extent of her knowledge of German culture.

Waldy remained on the floor of my grandmother's house in New York for over thirty years, an amusing fixture we kids could always count on seeing when we came for a visit. When Grandma died, Waldy relocated to my parents' house in New York, and then in Florida, where he would again take up his position on the floor and stand patiently for another twenty-five years. And when I sadly emptied out that house earlier this year I knew that there wasn't much that I wanted to take back with me to California, but I knew I wanted Waldy.

Waldy is still looking good for his age, but is not without his imperfections. I remember that long ago one of his paws had been broken off, although who the culprit was will forever remain a mystery. I only know it wasn't me. That paw had been glued back on, probably by Dad, who had done such a fine job that it took more than a casual glance for me to find the tell-tale crack that identified Waldy's front right paw as the injured one. He also has a slight chip over his left eye, but all in all he looks just fine, especially when you consider he is approaching seventy years old.

Although Waldy has only recently arrived in my home, I know that someday he must move on. And with that in mind I have already begun the process of identifying and selecting an appropriate person in the family, someone from the next generation, who will, when the time comes, carry Waldy even further into the future, a future that many of us will not experience, but can only imagine.

For now, though, Waldy seems quite content in his new home. As for me, I enjoy having him here, and I hope he stays with me for a while.

Leonard Stegmann

Clutch Performance

You've heard, no doubt, of a "Bucket List." That is, an enumeration of things we'd like to see or do before we die. For several years now I've had in my head what I call my Anti-Bucket List. It is made up of the things that, as I grow older, I expect I'll never see or do again.

For the longest time, and to my credit I suppose, there was only one thing on the list. I couldn't imagine eating Jujyfruits candy ever again. It was about ten years ago that I was chewing a wad of two or three or more of the tar-like sweet when I pulled off one of my crowns. I made a quick trip to the dentist, who glued me back together, and I was again as good as new.

Or so I thought. It was only *three days later* when I was again eating Jujyfruits, and this time I pulled off a crown from the *other* side of my mouth. It was embarrassing, to say the least, to return to the same dentist and tell him the same story. And that was the last time I've ever had any Jujyfruits.

I've recently admitted to myself that I will never again climb to the top of Half Dome, and so added that to my Anti-Bucket List. I've done that hike three times in my life, most recently (which wasn't all that recent) with my wife. I just saw a television program that documented the journey of hikers making their way to the top of the famous Yosemite landmark. Just seeing those people gripping onto the thick metal cables and pulling themselves up the steep side of Half Dome just about gave me acrophobia. And I was sitting on my couch at the time! Last year I joked with my wife that we should recreate our long-ago hike for her 50th birthday. She said she'd rather go to a luxury hotel, preferably one with a spa. I didn't argue.

"Of course I smell it. You think I'm nose-blind?" This was me barking at my wife about two weeks ago. We had left our house on a Sunday morning to drive "over the hill" to see a movie. To go just about anywhere from our little town you must drive up a long, steep road to the top of the mountains that make up the spine of the San Francisco peninsula, and then back down the other side, to the movies, malls and other sites of civilization. Normally it's a quick ride up and over, but on this day, for only the second time in ten years, traffic had come to a near crawl.

And so the smell, which was caused by me attempting to find the perfect balance between clutch, brake and gas to keep my car moving at the slowest of speeds, preferably without rolling back into the car right on my ass. I knew that if traffic didn't begin to move, and soon, things would only get worse for my little two-seater clown car. As it turned out, traffic did not begin to move and things did indeed get worse.

The smell soon became but a minor issue, as I looked in the rear-view and saw that smoke was billowing from the rear of my car. That, incidentally is where the engine is kept on this tiny vehicle. Luckily, there was a space in the lane to my right and, after some frantic hand waving from my wife, I pulled over and parked the car on the shoulder. And that's where we sat for the next hour, waiting for the traffic to break.

Somewhere along the way a helpful policeman asked if we needed assistance. I explained that I had most likely burned out my clutch, and once traffic had cleared I would attempt to drive home. At that time I would either be able to or I would call Triple-A for a tow. The friendly policeman confirmed that I had a phone, wished me good luck and was on his way.

I was seventeen years old when my dad gave me my first driving lessons. The family car was a 1962 Chevy Bel-Air, white if I remember correctly. It was also a stick shift, with the shifter on the column. This then, is what I would learn to drive on. At least that was the theory. My dad was a man who was endowed with many positive attributes. He was athletic, honest and quite generous by nature. What he wasn't though, was patient. And if I hadn't known that before the driving lessons began I certainly did after.

I spent many miserable hours bucking in that old car and being yelled at, sometimes while my two younger brothers giggled in the back seat. It wasn't, however, all my fault. Even during the times when I had shifted and worked the clutch just right, the old clunker wouldn't go into gear. I still remember Dad banging on the gear shifter with the palm of his hand, eventually succeeding in slamming the thing into second gear. Happily, Dad soon sold that Chevy, and I passed my driver's test in its replacement, the 1964 Comet that was the new family ride.

Fourteen years later I learned how to drive a stick shift. I had seen a car that I had liked and, although it had a manual transmission, I bought it on the spot. (It was a Pinto, but don't tell anyone.) The owner was nice enough to drive it to my house, where it sat in the driveway for two days. Finally I decided it was now or never, and I lurched that Pinto around the neighborhood until I learned how to drive it.

Since that day, over thirty years ago, every car I have owned has had a manual transmission. In fact, I wouldn't ever think of buying one that didn't. There were two reasons for this: driving a stick was simply more fun, especially in the sportier cars, like my Mustang GT. Also, there is just that much more power when you're climbing a hill or need a little extra speed. My wife and I generally both drive little Japanese cars with the same size engine. I'm always amazed how sluggish hers performs, with the automatic transmission, compared to mine. Okay, perhaps there are three reasons I always get a manual transmission. Could I still be trying to prove something to my dad? Or to myself? Geez, I hope not.

The traffic cleared, the smoke finally stopped and I was able to limp my car back home. It did, in fact, need a new clutch, which is not that surprising for a car with 100,000 miles. Still, I knew that I had burnt that clutch with that slow grind up the hill. And I came to a decision.

As I sat there waiting for the traffic to clear I watched the other people who were stuck in their cars, slowly creeping up the road. They were annoyed to be stopped, no doubt, by what we later found out was a major accident. Still, they just sat there relaxed; talking, drinking coffee or listening to the radio. They were not engaged in some mechanical battle between foot pedals and a gear shifter. Their cars didn't smell, as did mine, nor did they look like they had just burst into flames.

I'd like to keep my little car a while longer, because it really is a lot of fun. Yet, I know the inevitable is fast approaching and I'll have to buy a new one fairly soon. And I know that for the first time since the 1970's I'll be buying a car with an automatic transmission. And at that point I'll also know that, like eating Jujyfruits and climbing Half Dome, owning a car with a stick shift is something I'll never do again. And so, and probably with a sigh, I'll add it to my ever-growing Anti-Bucket List.

Leonard Stegmann

A Fish Story

It's an image I haven't forgotten over the last fifty years, and at this point I'm fairly certain that I never will. It was a large turtle and it was hanging from a tree, strung up by his tail and slowly twisting as he swatted the air with his front legs, futilely trying to escape. A house was just a few feet away, although nobody was visible. I tried to imagine why somebody would do such a thing to a turtle. Dad thought that perhaps they were trying to "work the fight out of him." I realize now that, whatever the excuse, it was just another in the endless line of human cruelties.

And so we floated by, Dad working the oars to the small rowboat he had rented for a few hours. Fishing from a boat was something of a treat, as we almost always cast our lines from the shore of some local lake. It was strange that it would be just me and Dad in the boat. Normally when we went fishing there were four of us: me, my two brothers and Dad.

In addition to always fishing from the shore, we also never used bait. Dad had taught us how to fish using lures. And as such, we almost never, ever caught anything. Time and time again we'd return home to report to Mom that, although the three of us had fished for hours, we had nothing but a sunburn and a bad smell to show for it.

Yes, the three of us. Dad himself never got much of a chance to fish, occupied as he was untangling his sons' wayward casts from the overhanging branches and nearby shrubs. Or, on a particularly unlucky day, he might spend half an hour cutting out a fishing line "bird's nest" from one of our reels. No, Dad didn't get to fish much.

But on this particular day, with just the two of us, Dad not only got to fish quite a bit, he even caught one. I, on the other hand, was having my usual luck; that is, none whatsoever. Finally the afternoon shadows began to find us out near the center of the small lake, and Dad told me to try one more cast and then we'd head in.

And so I did, and as I reeled in I began to think about my plans for the evening, never expecting the results of my closing cast to be any different than the previous sixty. But they were:

"You caught one!" Dad said, as he reached into the water and pulled out an honest-to-god fish.

Right away I could see something was not right. I may not have caught many fish in my angling career, but I'd *seen* them caught many times. I'd seen how a hooked fish with squirm around in the sun and flop around on the ground. This fish was different. I'm pretty sure he wasn't actually dead when Dad pulled him in, but he did seem to be kind of, I don't know, tired.

Also, the fish had not taken the lure, but rather had been hooked in the gill. Now, as you know from the opening paragraph, I've been around for a while now, and yet I haven't to this day ever again heard of a fish being caught in this manner. Clearly something was…fishy. Still, I ignored this feeling and we returned home, happy and proud to report to Mom that we had *each* caught a fish. Although, as they were both small, we had thrown them back into the lake.

It was years later, when I was in my twenties remembering that day, that it hit me. Wasn't it strange that I would go through the whole day not catching anything, and then catch a fish on what had been declared the last cast of the day? And even stranger, how the hell does a fish get himself hooked by his gill? Was he just standing around, minding his own business, when my lure came by and whoops? Was it possible that Dad had kept the fish that he had caught and then, at the end of the day, quickly, and inaccurately, slipped my hook into the fish even as he was loudly declaring that I had "caught one"?

Four decades passed from the time I came up with my theory until Dad died. I thought about that day once in a while, but never asked him if he had done it. I'm not sure why I didn't. Part of it, no doubt, is that it would have been yet another in our lifetime of awkward conversations. Also, I suspected he wouldn't have remembered putting that fish on the hook even if he had. I suppose that, in the end, I didn't ask him because, although I may have been a little disappointed if he *had* put that fish on my hook, I would have been even more disappointed if he hadn't.

Leonard Stegmann

An Immodest Proposal

I sure am glad that I'm not single and planning on getting married in the near future, and it's not because of any of the myriad reasons that just passed through your brain. No, it's because from what I've seen in recent weeks the proposal bar has been set outrageously high, and frankly, I no longer think I could compete.

Spike and I both enjoy oysters. One of our favorite spots to get them is on the wharf in Monterey. So just about sixteen years ago I took Spike down there for some oysters, and when I handed one to her it held, of course, a massive five-carat (It's called poetic license, Chum, so back off.) diamond ring. I watched carefully to make sure she didn't swallow the damn thing, and just like that we were engaged.

Pretty creative, huh? Well, I thought so at the time, but with what I've observed lately, if I tried a mundane stunt like that today I'd be afraid of being greeted with a smirk and sarcastic, "Are you kidding me with this?" Allow me to present two examples.

I just saw that the daughter of an old (as most of them now are) friend of mine recently got engaged, and the happy couple has the most delightfully unique photographic evidence to prove it. It seems the first time this couple ever kissed, nearly two years ago, it was in one of those photo booths. You know, where you close that little curtain and take four pictures in quick succession. (I was going to say "for a quarter," but really, do you need any more evidence of my decrepitude?)

So the guy gets his girl into one of these booths and, as the lights flash for each photo, he presents her with a ring and pops the question. What's amazing is that the four photos that result clearly tell the story. First the couple is looking at the camera, then he presents the ring, then she expresses joyful surprise and finally the newly-engaged pair seal it with a kiss. How he timed it so perfectly, whether by luck or careful planning, I can't say. The result, however is a simple yet remarkable record that they'll cherish forever.

I recently travelled to Peru, and while there I met a nice couple. They were somewhat younger than me, and by "somewhat" I mean a tremendous amount. And so, while our five-mile hike on a muddy trail through the Amazon had put me in the mood for a week-long nap, apparently it was just a warm-up for these hearty kids. When we parted company they headed out for a four-day trek over the rugged Inca Trail.

I wasn't there to witness the proposal, of course. I can't be sure, but I think I was in my hotel restaurant at about that time, scrarfing down breakfast at the complimentary buffet. I was fortunate enough to see the video on Facebook, however, and a sweeter scene I can't imagine.

It was at the end of their hike, and obviously the guy had asked a friend to video tape the event. It was morning, and the sun was just breaking over the top of the jagged Peruvian peaks. As the girl gazed over the magnificent view of Machu Picchu and the surrounding mountains, the guy chose that exact moment to drop to his knee and ask his question. This was followed by exclamations of surprise, a few tears and copious amounts of hugging.

I can't say that everything was perfect, although I'd be at a loss to imagine how he could have done it any better. Perhaps if a choir of angels had descended from on high singing Hallelujah. Short of that, though, it was quite a proposal. He had carried the ring on a four-day hike. They were gazing down on Machu Picchu, one of the most impressive sights in the world. The sun was just coming up over the mountains. And then he asked her to be his wife. Whew.

And so I imagine some guy standing there watching all of this, or perhaps seeing the video on Facebook. Maybe he, too, was planning on proposing to his girlfriend, but how could he ever top this performance? The pressure would be enormous. What was he supposed to do now, go to some wharf and hide a ring in her oyster? I don't think so.

Leonard Stegmann

You Won't See Me

❧❧❧❧❧

I toyed with the idea of not revealing the identity of the two young men in the following story until the end. And then I realized, it's a funny story, no matter who it happened to. The fact that the stars of the below tale happen to be John Lennon and Paul McCartney makes it a little more interesting, no doubt, but really, it could have happened to anybody and been just as amusing.

At one time during their youth, Lennon and McCartney lived only about a mile away from each other. This was quite convenient, not to mention a boon to music history, as Lennon would often walk to McCartney's home, where they would spend the day writing songs. When they were finished, usually late at night, Lennon would make the mile trek back to his own house.

It's common knowledge that the young John Lennon needed to wear glasses, without which he could barely see a thing. He was also in the habit of removing those glasses when there were girls around, or even when he thought there *might* be girls around. It's often been said that Lennon could hear all those screaming girls in the audience just fine; he just couldn't *see* them.

One day he showed up for his regular visit at his partner's home, and immediately asked McCartney a question.

"Paul, what time did I leave here last night?"

"About 11:30," answered Paul.

It seems it had happened again. On his walk home Lennon had been surprised that, even at that late hour, a neighborhood family was sitting on their front lawn, playing cards. And it wasn't the first time he had witnessed this rather odd behavior.

And so that night McCartney escorted his friend on his walk home. As they approached the house in question, Lennon pointed out that there was that family again, playing cards on their front lawn, even though it was close to midnight.

"John, put on your glasses." said McCartney. "That's a nativity scene."

Leonard Stegmann

A Dead-On Analogy For Sexagenarians

We're a funny generation, we Boomers. The oldest of us is now nearing seventy, and you still hear us talking about all the things we plan to do "down the road." It's hard to say from where this inability to face reality has come, although you probably wouldn't be far off to suggest that it arrived many years ago, riding giddily on the backs of an infinite number of THC molecules.

It was just around the time of my 60th birthday, and not coincidentally, I'm sure, that I came up with this amusing little analogy. It's proven to be quite entertaining for me, as well as educational for my aging hippie compatriots.

It's a sports analogy, but one so simple it can be understood by the fans and non-fans alike. The sport I chose is football, but it works equally well for any that is divided into four quarters. It also assumes a lifespan of eighty years, which I understand is quite an assumption, and not something we are guaranteed. Still, it's the approximate estimate for us right now, plus it fits nicely into my analogy.

That Won't Do You Any Good

Figure there are four quarters to your life, as there are four quarters in football. The first quarter of the assumed eighty years would be made up of your first twenty years, ending on your twentieth birthday; the second quarter would bring you to your fortieth birthday (halftime!) and so on. And so if you follow this logic, and I know I'm giving myself a lot of credit using that word, then then third quarter ends on your 60th birthday and ipso fatso, the fourth quarter begins.

Even at this point, though, the full effect generally doesn't hit my contemporaries. They usually just stand there, looking at me with a puzzled expression all over their wrinkled face. And so I have to tell them a story.

Imagine you come home from wherever and rush to the TV, because you've been wanting to see a certain football game. But somehow you've mixed up the time, and when you turn on the television you realize it's the start of the fourth quarter. You can't believe it. And to make things worse, the game is a blow-out and the outcome is not in any kind of doubt.

And so, with a heavy sigh, you click off the television. Your wife, husband, dog, whatever, comes into the room and asks you why you aren't watching the game you've been jabbering about all day. And so you explain that you messed up the starting time, and the game has already entered the fourth quarter.

And then what do you say after that? Do you say it should be fun to watch this last quarter? Do you say, well at least I got home in time to watch a little of this lopsided game? No, you say:

"We might as well go to the mall, Dear. Forget this game. It's almost over."

And it's always when they hear the phrase, "It's almost over" that my analogy finally hits home. It's really a joy to see. Just the other day I told this story to my neighbor, who was born the same year as I, and you should have seen her reaction to the "it's almost over" phrase. Her face dropped like the ratings of *The Michael J. Fox Show.*

"I, I, never thought of it like that," she stammered.

Well, of course you didn't, my erstwhile flower child with the now-drooping petals. That's what *I'm* here for. To tell you that it's almost over.

The Watch in the Back of the Drawer

Even though she had given it to me thirty-eight years ago, I knew just where to find it. And there it was, in a box with some other memories, crammed in the back of a drawer in the garage. I pulled it out and just held if for a second or two, and then looked at the back and read the simple inscription: *To Lenny 5-25-75 Love, Heidi.* I wound the stem and it started ticking.

I remembered the day Heidi had given it to me, a gift for my college graduation. She was a bit apologetic at the time, telling me that she had actually wanted to give me a different pocket watch, a better one, but it was out of stock. I didn't care. I thought it was a perfect gift, the kind that the recipient could hang onto for years and years. I was right.

I had met Heidi only eight months earlier, when I was teaching a section of Psychology 101 during my last year of schooling ever. I was a senior, she was a freshman. I had finished grading her most recent quiz and called her into the hallway to go over it. As I approached her and began to speak I ran my fingers through my hair. I thought it made me appear to be highly intelligent, a deep thinker of the first order. She later told me it reminded her of Columbo.

One weekend Heidi and I took the five hour bus ride from our college town to my parents' home on Long Island. Sick and wiped out from schoolwork, I had just given a presentation for my History of Psychology class, a presentation that had gone horribly wrong. By the time we arrived we were both physically exhausted, and we went to my childhood bedroom and fell right to sleep.

There were two beds in the room, and we each took one. The beds weren't even next to each other, but perpendicular. I would later find out that when my mother came home from work she was shocked that we, an unmarried couple, would be sleeping in the same bedroom. It would be the last time we would on *that* particular weekend.

We both woke up feeling much better. The next day we went into the city to see the musical *Grease* on Broadway. I can't begin to remember how I had gotten the tickets so quickly, or how I was able to pay for them. Heidi was excited to be seeing the play, but when we sat in the plush theater seats she was dismayed to find that she had forgotten her glasses. "My first Broadway play and I can't see it," she said sadly. And that was the last time she mentioned it. She enjoyed the play thoroughly.

Two months after I had graduated and returned home, in July, I made the long drive north to see Heidi, who was spending the summer at her mom's house. I'm not sure what type of romantic/erotic rendezvous I had in mind, but I found out quickly that it wasn't meant to be. As we hugged on the couch, and I attempted to kiss her, I knew things had changed. She was using words like "forever" while at the same time letting me down just about as gently as a person could. She was like a skilled and compassionate executioner – I never felt a thing.

We might have spoken a time or two on the phone after that, but I never did see Heidi again. Three months after my getting tenderly but unmistakably dumped I moved to California, and I would never again be in contact with her.

Over the years I tried to locate Heidi, but always without success. Then the Internet came into being, but still I couldn't find her. I feared the worst, but about eight months ago Heidi turned up on Facebook. Her photo was not immediately recognizable. I had last seen her when she was nineteen, and she was now fifty-five. But the combination of her hometown and our college were all the clues I needed.

I laughed to myself when I read some of her "likes." Politically she leaned way to the right, liking such Fox News stalwarts as Glenn Beck and Bill O'Reilly. Apparently she was also a fan of several Jesus-themed websites and churches and, perhaps most disturbing of all, she was a Yankees fan. I fantasized about the day when I would talk to her again, sometime down the line, and I would reference her dubious choices and tease her with the prepared line, "Boy, I let you out of my sight for forty years and look what happens!"

She liked other websites and organizations as well. I noticed she seemed to be particularly supportive of groups that combat cancer, particular breast cancer. My concern was aroused when Heidi posted a new photo of herself looking thin and haggard, but with a big smile on her face. Not only was she no longer the nineteen year old girl I had known, but she looked older than even her fifty-six years. Then two months ago she wrote that she was supporting a particular organization because "I'm battling Stage Four breast cancer."

I didn't contact Heidi. It seemed strange and somehow unfair, to get in touch with her after all these decades when she was so desperately ill. I *did* keep my eye on her Facebook page, however. I read as some of her friends complimented her on how nice her hair had grown back in. And I remembered her long blond hair as it whipped around her face as we stood on the wind-blown observation deck of the Empire State Building all those years ago.

About two months ago Heidi's Facebook photo changed again. The gaunt, smiling woman had been replaced by a simple and beautiful picture of a dove in flight. I checked back on a regular basis, but no additional information was posted. Finally last night I did a Google search on Heidi and found just one item: her obituary.

It was an inexpensive watch, and so I was surprised that it still was working after all these years. I put it up to my ear to listen to the ticking, read the inscription on the back one more time, placed the watch back into the box and returned it to the back of the drawer.

Leonard Stegmann

Campbell's "Pork" & Beans

Mom was alright. Even though she wanted it for herself, if you happened to be in the kitchen when she poured that can of Campbell's Pork and Beans into the saucepan, and if you were the first to find it, she'd let you eat that tiny piece of pork that was always hidden somewhere among the beans. Like I said, Mom was alright.

Did I say pork? What it was, and continues to be, is more a bit of fat, the sole purpose of which, it seems to me, is to protect the Campbell's folks from having to have only the word "beans" on their red and white label. I got a little nostalgic the other day when I opened a can, and you know, I never even found that tiny scrap of fat. It must have been an oversight on my part; I'm certain that Campbell's is unfailingly vigilant about putting that tiny glob in each can. It's like some glutinous, artery-clogging Crackerjack prize.

What I don't understand is how they get away with calling it Pork & Beans in the first place. Oh, I suspect that a hundred or so years ago when flatulent cowboys sat around the campfire, it truly was pork and beans, with big hunks of glistening pig floating around in there with all them beans. Why, if the cook had even once dared to serve beans with just a single, dime-sized morsel of fat, well, I have no doubt he would have been lassoed, tied to his own chuck wagon and dragged around the cactus-strewn prairie for a few miles. And deservedly so.

Originally I thought that they are legally compelled to call it Beans and Pork, as beans, being the major (and practically the only) ingredient, should be listed first. Then I realized that this is only required on the list of ingredients, not in the name of the product itself. (The three main ingredients, incidentally, are water, beans and, of course, America's national beverage: high fructose corn syrup.)

Still, if you bought a can of, say, Lobster and Wild Rice, and got home to find only a can of rice with but a tiny speck of lobster not large enough to fill a molar, well, I bet you'd be plenty peeved. And yet we've been putting up with this Pork and Beans scam since I was a kid, and probably a lot longer than that.

So Campbell's, why don't we do this: Let's just drop the whole charade, do away with that piece of "pork," and just call your product Beans. Or better yet, Barbeque Beans. It certainly would be more honest, and there would be other benefits besides. For example, based on the quantity in each can, I would estimate that you barely use one whole pig per half a million cans, or so. So admittedly, even if you eliminated the pork from your product you'd probably save only one pig's life a year. It doesn't seem like much to you, I know, but I'm sure *he'd* appreciate it.

That Won't Do You Any Good

Weight Loss Scam

Aren't you tired of wasting your money on products that make all these phony claims? I know I am. Case in point: you might remember me talking a few months ago about this new kitchen-top appliance in which you could make all sorts of nutritious drinks. You'd lose weight, they promised, an added bonus to your newly acquired radiant good health.

Well, listen up. I've been making and drinking these health drinks every morning for months and I don't think I've lost a pound. I can't be sure, since that fancy-ass digital scale we sprung for last year has long stopped working, but I did put on my suit to go to a wedding this weekend and it was *not* a comfortable feeling.

Let's just look at yesterday as an example of how this supposedly miraculous device has failed me. I woke up and immediately made my morning drink, as usual. The ingredients included kale, carrots, broccoli, a peach, a few grapes and a smattering of sunflower and flax seeds, as recommended in the booklet that came with the thing. I added some water, whipped it up and drank it down.

So far, so good, I thought to myself. I was really proud that I was improving my eating habits, and so decided to reward myself with one of those chocolate chip muffins that Spike keeps stashed in the refrigerator. To my credit I was conscious of all the calories contained in a single muffin, so

I cut one in two, put a few gobs of peanut butter and jelly on one half and put the other half back in the refrigerator. Then I ate the half muffin, opened the refrigerator, got the other half, put peanut butter and jelly on that one and ate it. Which was fine, since I'd already had my daily kale and broccoli.

Spike and I went for a walk on the beach and, knowing we had burned a few calories, went to McDonald's for lunch. Washing down my Big Mac and fries, I proudly noted the Diet Coke I was drinking and again became a little angry that my little blender had done nothing to take some weight off me, despite my having followed the recipes religiously for over six months. Perhaps the device was in some way defective?

So that evening I tinkered with the blender a bit as I prepared our dinner. We couldn't decide on whether to have the leftover chili or just make some hot dogs, and so we compromised and I made chili dogs. Before putting the dogs onto the bread, though, I made sure I added a thick slice of cheddar cheese. Now I can't say for certain that I tasted, or even saw, that cheese once the hot dogs were covered with mustard, relish, onions and chili, but it was just a nice feeling to know it was there.

Later that night we were watching a movie when I decided it was time for a snack. After all, some experts say it's better to eat five or six times a day, which sounds like a sensible plan to me. On top of the refrigerator there was an assortment of fruit, including apricots, bananas, plums and peaches. *Inside* the refrigerator there was an assortment of Nestle Drumstick ice cream cones. I grabbed a chocolate.

That Won't Do You Any Good

I woke up this morning and again created one of my supposedly weight-shedding concoctions. This one contained spinach, beets, a mango and some walnuts. I gulped it down, again wondering if I was wasting my time. Perhaps I should even write to the company and demand my money back. Yeah, I was going to do just that, perhaps a little bit later while I was having my coffee and donuts.

Leonard Stegmann

Brownies

I really must stop being shocked by the concept that people get older. Now, I hadn't seen Benny for almost forty years, and yet I was still taken aback by the grey-haired, albeit distinguished, gentleman who stared back at me from atop his Facebook page.

I had gotten to know Benny through my college roommate Ray, who had grown up with Benny. In fact it would only be a year after the event I am about to describe that Benny and I would become housemates, and thus closer friends.

Benny was a nice enough guy, but also something of a prankster. That's why it was a bit of a surprised when he called Ray and I one evening and invited us over. He had just made some brownies, and would we like some? We were on our way as soon as we hung up the phone.

Once at Benny's house, he directed us into the kitchen, where a pan of brownies was waiting on top of the stove. Ray and I each reached for one, and then Ray looked up at me with mischief in his eyes.

"Do you want to just eat the whole pan?" he asked conspiratorially.

I didn't think that would be the right thing to do, and so declined. I had been brought up to share. And so, in the end, Ray had three brownies and I had two.

Two hours later I hesitantly made my way down the stairs to the basement pub where Ray worked part-time as a bartender. I asked Ray if he was feeling okay, and he said he was feeling fine. That would change within the half-hour.

Now, at this point I hardly need to type the words to let you know what was going on. Benny had, of course, baked his brownies with a healthy dose of Ex-Lax. I had felt the results first, and figured out what had happened. Ray would feel the effect later, and more intensely.

It was about two in the morning when the striking of a match woke me up. I looked across the room to see an obviously suffering Ray propped up on his elbow, smoking a cigarette.

"That prick Benny," was all he said from inside the glow of the cigarette. And then he was up and running to bathroom, and not, I assumed, for the first time that evening.

Even now, decades later, I struggle to understand how Ray and I could have fallen so totally for a trick that now seems so painfully obvious. Benny, a known trickster, had, completely out of character, invited us over for brownies. And he had eaten none himself. I'm only grateful that I hadn't agreed to Ray's suggestion to eat the entire pan. (Although, admittedly, it would have made a better story, and a poignant morality tale about the nature of gluttony as well.)

And now there he sat, suit and tie, gray-haired and surrounded by his grandchildren. And you know, it gave me such a feeling of nostalgia and warmth to connect again with him after all these years. It's unfortunate that Benny lives three thousand miles away, because I'd enjoy getting together with him, perhaps for dinner. I could easily imagine him coming by for some wine and one of my famous chicken parmigiana dinners. And, of course, I'd make brownies for dessert.

That Won't Do You Any Good

How Much Is That Dollar in the Window?

It was very generous of Jimmy, really. All Chalky White had asked for was three thousand dollars for each family of his murdered workers, and here was Jimmy coming up with five. It was a nice gesture, and might have served him well in future dealings with Chalky, had not Nucky put a bullet into Jimmy's forehead a few scenes later. Spoiler alert! Oh wait, I'm supposed to say that *before* I give away the plotline, right? My bad.

Still, as I watched the exciting second season unfold, I couldn't help but wonder exactly how magnanimous was Jimmy actually being. I mean, the program takes place in 1920. Five thousand dollars today is just a drop in the bucket, especially when it's to compensate for the death of a loved one. But just how much was five thousand dollars worth back then, nearly a century ago?

That's why I find the inflation dollar calculator such a useful tool. Time and again when I hear a dollar amount mentioned from a different time I rush to the calculator (which you, too, could easily find online if you weren't such an incurious load) and see what amount we're actually dealing with.

Why, just this weekend I watched the episode of *The Honeymooners* when Ralph, his visiting friend and their wives have to scrounge up forty bucks to pay the check at the high-end restaurant that none of them could afford. "I've got nine dollars!" chimes in the ever-helpful Alice.

Forty dollars! you scoff. Four people ate at a fancy-ass restaurant and it only cost forty bucks? Man, I wish I lived back then! But do you, really? A quick visit to the dollar inflation calculator would tell you that in 1956 a dollar had the same buying power as $8.33 today. And so Ralph's meager dinner bill was actually the equivalent of about $333.00 today! And so we see that he really had no business being in that restaurant, especially on his paltry bus driver's salary.

And what about in times closer to our own? In *Lost in America*, Albert Brooks convinces his wife that they have enough equity in their home to sell it, buy a motorhome and live comfortably for the rest of their lives just driving around and "finding America." Albert figured they could raise about $190,000 in cash, buy a perfectly fine motorhome for $45,000, leaving them a nest egg of a cool $145,000 in cash.

So, was Albert right? Was this enough for the couple to live on comfortably for the rest of their lives? Well, a quick check of the calculator tells me that Albert's 1985 fortune of $145,000 would today be the rough equivalent of $305,000. A tidy sum, to be sure, but is it enough for two young people to live on for the next forty or fifty years? I think Albert made a mistake on this one. Not to mention his *other* mistake, which was making the first stop on his adventure the gambling mecca of Las Vegas. Spoiler alert! Damn, did it again.

When, I was a mere wisp of a lad—wait, strike that. I was *never* a mere wisp of anything. Let's try again: When I was a kid I used to cut the neighbor's lawn each Saturday morning. I would be paid a dollar for the front lawn and a dollar for the back. It seems crazy now, but was it? When I put these numbers into the calculator I find that a dollar in 1965 was the rough equivalent of seven dollars today.

So maybe it makes a little more sense, but I have to tell you, I occasionally have kids come to the door looking to cut my overgrown lawn. And without fail, when I tell them the delightful story of how I used to cut lawns for a dollar, and that it's equal to seven dollars today, they invariably give me a dirty look as if I were quite mad. The look is usually delivered over their shoulder as they are walking away from me, and is sometimes, I suspect but cannot prove, accompanied by a simple yet obscene hand gesture.

And so the next time you're watching a TV show or reading a book set in a different time in American history, why not get off your lazy duff and check out its value on the dollar inflation calculator? Trust me, it will help put the story into perspective for you. Oh, and if any of you are actually still out there reading this, bless your hearts, the five thousand dollars that Jimmy gave to each of the victim's families was roughly equivalent to $57,000 today. This is certainly a small price for the loss of a loved one, but really, it's not too bad. No, not too bad at all.

That Won't Do You Any Good

An Acre of Sand

ชีชีชีชีชี

It's as heart-rending a task as you'll ever do, going through your parents' belongings as you empty out their house. There are photos of Dad in shoulder pads, looking young and lean and outrageously happy with his high school teammates. And Mom, stylishly dressed in her classic forties outfit and a smile, both of which say, I'm ready to take on the world. And yet no photo, no faded bit of clothing or shiny piece of jewelry brought me closer to tears than the deed to that acre of sand.

Throughout the house I found articles that were purchased because of some attraction that the buyer had felt, yes, but also with the unspoken hope that sometime in the future these items might increase, perhaps even skyrocket, in value. There are the Hummels and the Lladro and that Norman Rockwell collector plate, a plate that was purchased in 1981 and now, three decades later, sells on eBay for about four bucks.

It was quite out of character, and to this day I can't explain it. It was 1972 and my parents saw an ad in the newspaper advertising land for sale in New Mexico. Nobody in our family had ever been to New Mexico, nor did any of us have any intention of going there. Still, my parents not only sent in a check for $300 for a half acre of land somewhere near a town called Deming, but soon changed their minds, adding an additional $300 and thus purchasing a full acre.

It must have been a time when the financial crush had finally eased a bit, and my parents decided they should put something away for the future. Why they chose land over the traditional bank account I'll never know, but I have no doubt they thought that this non-liquid asset might be something of value to leave to their children, when the time came.

And inevitably the time did come this year. I went online and was able to find the tract of land that included my parents' long-ago purchase. One website estimated that the value of the half-acre lots was now about $600 each. And as anybody can tell you, simply doubling in value over forty-plus years is a piss-poor return on any investment, and that seems especially true for real estate. But that's not the entire story.

You see, my parents had acquired the land in 1972 dollars, and their $600 purchase was actually the equivalent of about $3300 today. So, when you adjust for inflation, over the last four decades the land had actually *lost* about two-thirds of its value. And this is what made me so remarkably sad.

It wasn't because the land that I now owned was basically worthless. It was the thought of those two people, still in their forties, trying to win a game in which they never stood a chance. Who knows what kind of sleazebags originally concocted the scheme to unload their worthless lots on unsuspecting and unsophisticated working people thousands of miles away. Whoever they were, the numbers say the sales worked out for them just fine.

But that's seldom the case for the ordinary, blue collar people like my parents, who were just hoping to finally get a little bit ahead, and maybe even make something of a score for once in their lives. And yet in the end my parents *did* win the game. They left me with a priceless trove of happy memories and fond looks back. And if they also left a worthless acre of sand somewhere on the outskirts of Deming, New Mexico, well, it turns out that really doesn't matter much at all.

Leonard Stegmann

It'll Be Just Like Starting Over

In one way, I suppose it's not so very odd that a dentist would go to an auction and buy a tooth. Especially since this particular dentist already had a prized collection of dinosaur teeth. This tooth, however, didn't come from the mouth of a dinosaur. It came from John Lennon.

Three years ago Dr. Michael Zuk bought one of John Lennon's teeth for $33,000. The tooth had been put up for sale by Lennon's old housekeeper, who is now over 90. And if you think the story so far is a tad bit strange, well, stick around. It's about to get better.

You see, Dr. Zuk has stated that he plans to extract some DNA from the famous tooth, and then attempt to clone John Lennon. He would then raise the child as his own. The cloned person would not be John Lennon himself, of course, but an exact genetic duplicate of the rock legend.

Many people have expressed moral outrage at the plan. I find people tend to express moral outrage at just about anything. As for me, I just feel sorry for the kid. Growing up is hard enough; who needs *that* kind of pressure?

That Won't Do You Any Good

Dr. Zuk has said that he would let the child find his own way in life, but somehow I suspect the temptation to do otherwise would be too great, probably for any of us. I imagine more than a few conversations similar to this might take place around the Zuk household:

"So Johnny, how was school today?"

"Dad, I told you not to call me that. My name is Billy!"

"Oh, sorry. So, uh, Billy, what did you study in school today?"

"Oh, we learned some history, and I had a lot of fun in shop class. I made an ashtray."

"Oh, that's nice. Did you by chance have music class?"

"Dad, you know I hate music. I like shop. And sports. I want to be a professional football player someday!"

"Yes, yes, that's fine son, but don't you ever find yourself humming something, or maybe hearing a song in your head?"

"Nope. That never happens."

"Well, I'll just leave this pencil and paper lying here, you know, in case any lyrics should ever pop up."

"D-a-a-a-d!"

"I also put a guitar in your bedroom, and another one in the living room."

"D-a-a-a-a-d!"

"Oh, and maybe you should stop getting so many haircuts."

"D-A-A-A-A-A-A-D!"

I don't know. Those morally outraged people may have a point after all.

That Won't Do You Any Good

M&M Dreams

Last night I dreamt that I was buying some M&M's from one of those gumball-style machines. I turned the knob, lifted the little metal flap and M&M's suddenly came pouring out by the hundreds. They scattered onto the floor, and soon I was on my knees, grabbing handfuls of the candy and stuffing them into my pockets like they were gold nuggets.

Even in my dream I was a little concerned. I knew that M&M's didn't melt in your hands, and that they *do* melt in your mouth, but I didn't ever recall reading anything about what they do in your pants pockets. Also, there were still tons of them on the floor, and I wanted them all. The problem was there were two or three people nearby, and so I was not-so-patiently waiting for them to leave, so that I could continue picking up the candy from the dirty floor without them seeing, and judging, me.

It's not hard to figure out where this dream came from. We were at the mall on Sunday and I put two quarters in the M&M machine, just like in the dream. Unlike in the dream, however, they didn't come pouring out by the hundreds. In fact, I was amazed at how few M&M's I got for fifty cents.

Did I ever tell you that candy was only a nickel when I was a kid? (Only about a thousand times, Leonard.) Imagine, I could have gotten *ten bags* of M&M's back then for the same amount of money I had just spent on a few piddly candies. And to make matters worse, I shared them with Spike. (Giving her three out of eleven is still considered sharing, right?)

Today I went to the grocery store. Remembering Spike's admonishment to "don't forget the dessert" (as if I ever would) I bought one of those plastic containers jammed with cookies. Fifty of them for five bucks, and they are quite good besides. What's not to like?

When I got to the checkout and began to empty out my hand basket, the plastic container popped open and cookies came spilling out. As the cashier was ringing up my other items I frantically reached into the basket, grabbing handfuls of cookies to be put back into the container. I was aware that the spilled cookies were all lying directly on the bottom of the dirty plastic basket, and I rushed to get the job done before the cashier, or the customer behind me, saw what I was up to. I briefly thought that, if she saw me, the cashier might offer to take the contaminated cookies and send someone to get me a batch of non-befouled ones, but she never did.

As I shoved mittfuls of cookies into the container, still hoping not to be seen, I couldn't help but laugh. Wasn't this just like my dream? After all, I was grabbing items by the bunches, hoping that nobody noticed they had fallen onto a dirty surface, and that I intended to eat them anyway. And then I thought maybe I was stretching things a bit. After all, here at the store I was picking up cookies, while in my dream it had been M&M's.

I was back in my car and halfway home when it hit me; so hard, in fact, that a slight chill ran down my spine. The cookies that I had so frantically picked up, and which now rested in the bag on the passenger seat beside me, were not the usual chocolate chip cookies that I usually bought. This batch was a little different. This batch was made with…M&M's!

M&M's! Just like in my dream! Do you know what this means? Do you know what this *means*? Well, I'll tell you. It means that M&M's apparently play much too large a role in my life, that's what.

Leonard Stegmann

Nixon Resigns

I don't know why I'm always surprised when told that a certain amount of time has passed. After all, this is what time does. It passes. And yet when I heard that it has been forty years since the resignation of Richard Nixon I was again astonished.

It was the summer between my junior and senior years of college, and I was working as a busboy in Lake Placid, New York. It would prove to be an event-filled summer, four of which will always come to mind. One of the events, the death of Mama Cass Elliot, was sad. Two others—an arrest and the acquisition of a certain type of body lice--would involve me personally, and so be even sadder. The fourth event would prove to be the most historic, and that was the resignation of President Richard Nixon.

We, the younger generation, all despised Nixon, or at least we were supposed to. I never really could generate much of hatred for the man, but generally went along with the notion that his being forced out of office, and into disgrace, was a good thing. It would be another three decades before I would fully understand what it was like to truly abhor a sitting U.S. president.

Still, I knew that Nixon's quitting, much like the moon landing and the Beatles on Ed Sullivan, was a happening of historic proportions, and I wanted to see it. We had been told by the news people of the time that Nixon would address the nation that night, and while nobody could say for sure that he was going to resign, that would certainly be the way to bet.

And then there was my girlfriend Mandy. We had met in Lake Placid at the beginning of the summer and after a somewhat rough beginning (See "body lice" above) we had settled into a rather pleasant Adirondack romance. Mandy was a waitress, and worked in the same dining room as I did.

Just about all of the other waiters, waitresses and busboys had completed their dinner shift responsibilities and had headed back to the dorm, most likely to gather around their portable televisions to gleefully watch Nixon's farewell performance. Mandy, for some reason, hadn't yet finished up, and so I found myself getting more and more frustrated with her.

Now, here's where things get murky. I'm not quite certain why my heading back to the dorm was contingent on Mandy concluding her chores. I can think of only two possibilities: either I couldn't finish my job until she finished hers, or I was waiting for her so we could walk back to the dorm together. I'd like to believe that I was enough of a gentleman that the latter was the case. I suspect it was. I know one thing for sure: If it had been ten years earlier and the Beatles were on Ed Sullivan that night, Mandy would have been walking that dark, wooded path back to the dorm all by herself.

I couldn't shake then, and I can't tonight, the vague suspicion that Mandy was dragging her feet that night, purposely taking much longer at her job than she needed to. But why? Was there some reason she didn't want me to see Nixon resign? Was she being playful? Spiteful? Was she (gasp!) a secret Nixon-lover?

And now forty years have passed and it looks like I'll never know the answer. And if she did have a secret strategy to spoil my television viewing pleasure on that historic night, well, she failed. We arrived back at the dorm in plenty of time to adjust the antenna of my tiny black and white TV and watch Richard Milhous Nixon become the only president in history to resign from office. Mandy and I would resign from each other about a year after that.

That Won't Do You Any Good

Oh-Fer-Four

Growing up, my friends and I would play one sport or another nearly every day. For the most part the specific sport we chose to play was dictated by the seasons. We'd play endless games of baseball (and curb-ball) in the summer, and football in the winter. And basketball hardly ever.

I almost never played an organized sport. I did join Little League twice, once in second grade and once again in sixth. The first season I played I got one hit. No, not per game, but one hit for the entire season. It was a slow roller back to the pitcher that I somehow managed to beat out. It might even have been an error. I don't know, because I wasn't looking. Even today I don't know if it was a true hit, and I don't want to know.

But mostly we played baseball in the street, usually with only two kids on each team. "Invisible men" were very important in those games. I was never what anybody might describe as "athletic," but I had fun. And yet in the hundreds of games I played as a kid, the game I remember with the most pride took place many years later, when I was already in my thirties.

I had gone with a friend to his company picnic. Earlier in the day I had foolishly agreed to participate in a grueling game of ultimate Frisbee. It was a double whammy for me, because I didn't really have the physical stamina that this game requires, and also I never really learned how to throw a Frisbee. I was from the East Coast, dammit. We only played *real* sports there.

Later in the day there was a softball game, and I felt much more suited to play that. And so I did. Now, of course I don't remember if my team won or lost, but I'll never forget, apparently, my own personal performance. It went something like this:

Remember, except for my friend I knew nobody on either side in the game. And they didn't know me. And even though I've never been much of a power hitter, the first time I was up I connected and drove the ball deep into center field. It was caught, but I still felt a bit of pride. Sure it was an out, but it was so much less embarrassing than, say, hitting a dribbler to the shortstop or, God forbid, striking out. Especially in front of all those strangers.

My second at bat was a repeat performance. I hit the ball squarely and again sent the ball soaring out to centerfield, where again it was caught. Already I could feel a bit of respect flowing my way from both teams. This guy can hit.

I pulled the ball a bit during my third at bat. Again it flew out to the deep part of the outfield, but, unfortunately, it landed in the glove of the waiting left-fielder. And suddenly I was feeling, for the first time in my life, like a legitimate power hitter. Even though I hadn't even gotten to first base all day.

My fourth at bat is the one I'll never forget. I dug in to await the first pitch. And then I saw it. By this time the centerfielder recognized me, and he did something that I'd never before seen an outfielder do during one of my at bats, and never would again. He took a few steps back.

Well, I swung at the first pitch and sent the ball sailing to deep centerfield, almost to the exact spot where the centerfielder was waiting. He easily caught the ball, and so ended my last at-bat for the day.

Like I said, I don't remember if we won that game. I *do* know that I personally went 0-for-4. I had failed to reach base even once, and my batting average for the day was a worst possible .000. And yet this was the game I remember above all others. You see, that centerfielder had seen that it was me up at bat, and then he'd taken a few steps back.

Leonard Stegmann

Herman's Deli

I'm trying to get a clear picture of Herman in my head, and I'm not doing a very good job of it. Don't judge me too harshly though, since it was such a long time ago. I keep getting vague images of tall, swarthy, balding men who look like, oh I don't know, Paul Stookey? Salman Rushdie? Herman Franks?

Herman's Deli was just under a mile away from the house I grew up in. It was a straight shot up Broadway, and the first place a kid could spend some change once he hit "town." Herman's wasn't so much a place we kids would go if we needed something, it was more the place we would go if we wanted something to do. And happened to have a few coins in our pockets.

"Wanna go to Herman's?" we'd ask, and without so much as a verbal answer we'd be on our bikes headed north. Springtime was the high season for going to Herman's. That's when the weather was nice and, more importantly, the baseball cards came out. Five cards, and a slab of gum with the chewing consistency of a poker chip, all for a nickel. I can still remember the smell of a fresh, unopened pack of baseball cards, the perfect blend of sugar and cardboard. Mmmm.

Candy, of course, was more than enough of a reason to pedal the twenty minutes up to Herman's. What to get was always a topic of discussion on the ride up. For me it was often a toss-up between M&M's and a Hershey bar. And like the baseball cards, each cost only a nickel.

Sometimes there was a new product making its debut on Herman's dark, wooden counter. I remember the Sweet Tarts rage of 1963. How we could choose these offensive tasting tablets over a chocolate bar is beyond my comprehension today, but hey, we were kids. And it was only a few years later that the Great Razzles Bewilderment began. What the hell were these things anyway, we wondered, a candy or a gum? Say what you will about ol' Herman, where candy was concerned he lived on the cutting edge.

And it wasn't all about candy, either. Looking back, I can see that Herman had a knack for knowing exactly what we kids wanted. You could, for example, buy a balsa wood airplane for a dime. And unlike the wood and paper models you could spend days gluing together (which I never had the slightest desire to do) the assembly on these couldn't be easier. There were two steps: 1. Insert the wings through the slit in the body of the plane. 2. Throw.

There was a better plane though, and at half the price, although it was not always available. It was a small, plastic job which basically looked like a pair of wings attached to a hollow Bic pen housing. It came in a variety of colors (I preferred blue) and with a launching device which was basically a short, plastic stick with a rubber band attached. You'd loop the rubber band over the short hook on the bottom of the plane, pull back and let'er go. I'm telling you this thing *flew*!

As exciting and as much fun as this plane was, every kid knows there is always room for improvement. And so one day a couple of the neighborhood kids announced they were going to insert a firecracker in the plane, light it and launch it. A once-in-a-lifetime event like this, of course, will gather quite a crowd of kids. Who would want to miss something as incredible as this promised to be? No me, that's for sure.

The explosive-packed plane didn't fly into some kid's eye. It didn't land on somebody's roof and start a fire. What it did was fly a few feet, clearly hampered by the additional weight, and then explode in mid-air. We all chimed in with a collective, "Whoa," and thought this was pretty cool. Which it was, but had we been totally honest we would have admitted that the anticipation had outshone the actual event. It was something of a let-down. Looking back, though, I can see now that for we kids this was perfect training for life's approaching disappointments.

Occasionally Mom would send me up to Herman's to buy her a pack of cigarettes. First Chesterfields, and later, Parliaments. A pack cost twenty-eight cents, and was freely handed over to a ten year old child. Herman knew without a doubt that the cigarettes were for my mother. A few years later Herman toyed with the idea of requiring a note, but I think this concept never became more than a suggestion, rather than a hard-and-fast rule.

It was on the way to Herman's that one of the more dramatic episodes of my childhood occurred. We had only ridden about a block when I decided to show my friend a trick on my bicycle. The result was a sudden and unexpected planting of my face smack into the middle of Broadway. I broke off one of my teeth at the gum line, an incisor the chart I just looked up tells me, and so rode right home. An emergency visit to dentist introduced me to the first of what would be many painful root canals.

I must have been half-way to the street's tarry surface when I realized there would be no trip to Herman's on that particular day. A second later the broken tooth confirmed this, and that I certainly wouldn't be consuming a Hershey bar anytime soon. And that was too bad, really. Did I tell you they were only a nickel?

Leonard Stegmann

Getting a Needle

The anxiety would begin around the first week of August, and while not completely destroying the joys of summer vacation it would certainly put a crimp in them. And the intensity of the anxiety itself, which could vary from mild to severe, would be greatly affected by what the doctor had said the year before.

At these times I was always hugely relieved to hear the doctor say that I wouldn't be getting a needle until the following year. Oh, he didn't say "needle," exactly. He used quasi-medical terms like "booster," "inoculation" and "injection," but I knew what he meant. Nobody was going to be sticking a needle into my arm (or worse!) at the beginning of *this* particular school year.

And so, feeling much like the governor had phoned in a reprieve, I sprung out of the office, free and unpunctured, and returned to my regular non-threatened life. And while perhaps the prospect of getting a needle was never entirely gone from my mind, the knowledge that I wouldn't have to deal with it for a whole year provided a nearly absolute relief. A year seemed so far into the future that the doctor might as well have said I wouldn't need another needle until I was an old man in my thirties.

Inevitably, though, August would roll around, clouding up what had been up until then a glorious, fun-filled summer. It was then that I started to think about the approaching "injection," and became filled with dread. To this day I can't explain why I feared the needle so, nor can I understand why that fear would one day so suddenly and completely disappear.

Most years I entered the doctor's office not knowing if I would be getting a needle or not. It was during these times that I likened myself to a 19th century French prisoner who would not know the day of his execution until he heard the ominous knock on his cell door. Well, in hindsight maybe it wasn't as dramatically horrible as all that, but I was a kid and it sure felt that way.

One particular check-up, however, was different. It had been one year since the doctor had buckled my knees with relief by telling me I wouldn't need a shot until the following year. And now that time had arrived. I shuffled into the office, imagining an "Abandon All Hope" sign hanging above the door. At least I *think* I imagined it. I sat shakily in the chair as the doctor reviewed my file, waiting for him to find the year-old notation left by the previous doctor, and knowing that he inevitably would. "Get him!" I presumed it said.

I'm not a religious man, but I was something of a religious boy. And so I doubt that there was a person on Earth who, at the time, could have convinced me that my prayers hadn't been answered when, a few minutes later, the doctor looked up and said, "Well, no shots for you this year." (It was also my first hint that adults were perhaps not as perfect as they seemed to be, nor nearly as organized as they pretended they were.) In my joy and relief, I didn't know whether to hug the doctor or smack him across the face, but as I was nine years old, I did neither.

That Won't Do You Any Good

You Bed Your Life

✥✥✥✥✥

I've been running this around in my brain for a few hours now, and I still find it inconceivable. Is it truly possible that until yesterday I had never before in my ever-lengthening life purchased a brand new mattress? No, that can't be right, can it?

Now it goes without saying--but I'll say it anyway--that I've always had one. And that includes every stage of my life, from the high-end pillow-top Macy's job I've been sharing since getting married to the twin-sized, college era foam bags that had no doubt been baptized over the years with spilled wine, brown bong water and a colorful variety of bodily fluids I'd prefer to not write, or even think, about.

Well, no matter. That's all in the past. Today I can finally boast that I am now the proud owner (well, *half* owner) of my very first brand spanking new mattress *and* box springs, and I haven't even yet reached the age of social security eligibility. Little Leonard is growing up!

It was time. The mattress we were using had been purchased by Spike nearly twenty-five years ago. It had cost quite a bit, even back then, but at this point it

offered the support of a deadbeat dad and had been
flipped over more times than your sister. And so to
Sears.

And not to buy, mind you, but to "look around." See,
I've become quite the online guy. I've long believed
that all of life's answers could be found there, and the
perfect mattress (at a cheap price) was no exception.
But despite all the cyber advances we enjoy, you still
can't "feel" a mattress online. Yet. Did we want a plush
or a pillow-top or a firm or what? The only way to find
out to do some testing in the field. Or better, in Sears's
basement.

It was miracle of sorts, I think, that Spike and I agreed
on the firm. I though she'd be a plush chick for sure.
And so, a thank you to the friendly saleswoman and
back to the discount website to find just the right
(cheap) mattress.

The one I eventually zeroed in on was actually a firm
with a pillow-top. There were over 100 reviews on the
thing and they averaged out at a more-than-respectable
4 ½ stars. The average would have even been closer to
five stars, but there were a few one-star reviews mixed
in. Which I made the mistake of reading.

Some people, it seemed, really didn't like the mattress,
In fact, they downright hated it. I read the reviews and
two things stuck with me: One person bemoaned the
waste of $500 (gasp!) and the other who had typed this

ominous warning, in all caps, which read DON'T BUY A MATTRESS ON THE INTERNET!

Back at Sears we again tested out different mattress, Goldilocksing our way through row after row. This one was too hard and this one was too soft. And then, once again, another miracle; we both agreed on a mattress that felt *just right*.

I had also set my mind and my jaw against my usual modus operandi of prying the least amount of money out of my dusty wallet that I possibly could. I reasoned (for once, and it felt good) that at my current rate of mattress purchases, which clocked in at just about one a lifetime, I would be spending a great deal of time on this new one. With luck, I'd be sleeping, reading, boinking, eating and who knows what else on this mattress for many years to come.

And when that luck eventually runs out, as it always does, well, I might even be dying on this mattress. And hopefully, when that dreaded yet inevitable moment arrives, my spirits will be lifted just knowing that, even though I might be checking out to face the eternal void, I'll be doing so on a pretty snazzy pillow-top mattress.

Leonard Stegmann

With Five Popular Settings

Dammit, I must have thrown it out. Oh, hi there, didn't hear you come in. What you caught me squawking about is a box that I had saved—or thought I had saved—in my garage. I bought a new shower head a couple of weeks back and thought some of the description on the box might be amusing enough to share with you. And just a few minutes ago I find out that the box I saved was for my new telephone, not the shower head. Dammit.

I *do* remember the box had boasted that my new shower head came with "five popular settings." It made me laugh to think that I wasn't getting just any old settings, but the *popular* ones. I was pretty happy that I hadn't bought a shower head that came with any of those "unpopular" settings, and I wondered exactly what they could be. I suppose they might include the much feared Chinese torture drip setting, and perhaps even the dreaded flesh-ripping Extreme Stream setting. I'm sure glad I read the box first before I bought that shower head.

A friend advised that I could fix my old and clogged shower head by simply soaking it in vinegar. You know, if that worked on major purchases, like refrigerators or automobiles, I'd be soaking them in vinegar in a minute. But to go through all that for a shower head, instead of simply buying a new one, seemed excessively parsimonious, even for me. Go wild, I told myself. Spend the twenty bucks and shower like a king. And that's exactly what I did, and the improvement is dramatic. Besides, I believe I tried the vinegar trick on a shower head once before, with less than stellar results.

Years ago I was taking a shower in a hotel room in Nairobi. It was the first time I had used one of those "rain" shower heads. I found the experience delightful, and vowed to get one when I got back home. I eventually did, but didn't use it for very long. It had seemed quite exotic the first time, being as I was in a foreign land, in a room right next door to a rather boisterous gaggle of hookers. But back in everyday life it just wasn't functional. You need that water pressure, man, unless you're content to walk around all day with shampoo in your hair and a soapy film encasing your body.

And so now life is good, equipped as I am with both a new shower head and a new telephone. The total cost for both of these conveniences, incidentally, came to less than forty dollars. And like the new shower head, the phone also seems to be functioning quite well, at least so far. And if it gets to the point where it doesn't, well, maybe I'll try soaking it in some vinegar.

That Won't Do You Any Good

I Married a Hoarder

ఆఈఆఈఆఈ

"I'm not a hoarder!" insisted Spike, despite the veritable mountain of crap-filled plastic containers towering right before my eyes.

You see, they were coming in two days to install the new garage door, and had told us that all of our "possessions" needed to be pushed back eight feet, to allow the workman room. I now looked at the task ahead, and thought that it was roughly the equivalent of a pharaoh saying, "Oh, that pyramid is lovely, but can you move it ten feet to the left?"

"Do you put your car in the garage?" my dad had asked over the phone.

"Are you kidding?" I replied. "I can barely fit my bike in there.

Hours later and the chore was done. All of the junk had now been compressed into the rear half of the garage, a transformation that made the pile look even more daunting. The man arrived on schedule and the garage door was installed without a hitch. (Hitches cost extra.)

And so now the real job began. I said that getting a new garage door was the perfect time to organize the garage, and get rid of a lot of its contents. The fact that Spike readily agreed perhaps shows that she wasn't a true hoarder. After all, those sorry folks on TV have so much accumulated debris that they need to create narrow pathways that are barely wide enough to walk through. Then again, maybe Spike wasn't at this stage of hoarderhood, but at some point the TV show folks had to pass through Spike's stage to get to the mess they were in today, right?

There's a reason Spike did most of the work, and it's not because 90% of the rubbish was hers. Well, that's not the *only* reason. Most of the process would involve condensing the contents of the containers. You know, squeezing the innards of three boxes into two. Plus, Spike had to decide what she was going to keep and what she was going to jettison.

"Look, here's a brand-new stapler!" she said.

"Oh good, we can put it in the office closet with the other five," I answered, with perhaps the teeniest trace of sarcasm.

And so we began to haul long-forgotten objects out to the curb, where we hung a FREE sign on them. Giant wooden lattices I thought would be rotting in my garage until a week or so after my funeral were almost immediately taken by a particularly enthusiastic young man.

That Won't Do You Any Good

"Sir, I can't believe you knew I needed lattices!" he chirped. I felt warm all over.

Stuffed rabbits from the last dozen Easters, and other assorted fuzzy animals, were snatched up by a pudgy and cheery blonde women. Her smile got even wider when I brought out five more stuffed creatures. "Do you have a bag?" she asked. Sure, why not.

All day long we added to the pile at the curb, and all day long people came by to claim their free treasures. Finally just a few of the crappier items were left, but that was no problem. In addition to the Junkapalooza taking place at the end of our driveway we were planning to make a donation to a local charity when they arrived for a pick-up in a few days.

We'd start with an old school TV, an extra DVD player, some small appliances and about ten bags stuffed with clothes. (Three shirts of which were mine.) And finally we had scheduled a special garbage pick-up day for later in the week, where we are permitted to leave, in addition to our usual deposit, twelve containers of refuse and one "large item." Along with a recycle bin that is currently overstuffed for the first time in years.

And still, even with the pile of curbside freebies, the charitable donations and the industrial-sized garbage pick-up, we found that the remaining containers, books, suitcases and record albums still formed an impressive wall that stretched, in places, all the way to the garage ceiling. And so, when the task was finally completed, an exhausted but proud Spike looked at the still-huge pile of personal effects.

"Maybe I really *am* a hoarder," she laughed.

Of course you are, Sweetie, of course you are.

File Sharing: 1971 Style

Arthur and Howie agreed, and who was I to argue? I had wanted them to record me a cassette tape of *Retrospective: The Best of Buffalo Springfield*, but I was soon made to understand that this made no sense. After all, Buffalo Springfield had only recorded three albums in the two years they were together, and there hadn't been a bad song on any of the six sides.

"So why not have them all on one tape?" asked Howie.

Why not, indeed? And so the next time I saw Howie he handed me a 120 minute cassette. It seemed like an impossible dream, but here it was: Everything ever recorded by Buffalo Springfield, right there in the palm of my hand. I thanked him profusely, or at least I hope I did, and headed out to my car to pop my new tape into the boxy, fifteen-pound tape-player slash radio that my parents had given me for graduation.

I don't know which I found more exciting, that I now had the equivalent of all three Buffalo Springfield albums, or that I had gotten it for free. If I spent even a second feeling guilty about having possibly taken food out of Neil and Stephen's mouths, well, I don't remember.

Howie had recorded the albums in the order of release, as anybody would have expected him to. I leaned back in my car seat and pulled out of Howie's driveway to the opening notes of "Go and Say Goodbye," and drove around burning up 38 cent gasoline until the fading last strains of the simple and elegant "Kind Woman." Then I flipped the tape and started all over again.

I played the hell out of that tape all summer long, and then in September took it with me to my freshman year of college. The tape served me well right into my sophomore year, but alas, it is the nature of all things to wear down, and my cassette containing every song released by Buffalo Springfield was no exception. And so one day, without the slightest bit of a warning, the tape just broke. I was sad when that happened, perhaps sadder than one should be over the loss of something as mundane as a cassette tape, but we had, after all, spent many happy hours together.

Right now I can click over any number of music websites, type in 'Buffalo Springfield,' and listen to any song that was on my old tape, and as often as I want. Additionally, I can hunt down alternate renditions of these songs, unknown songs that were never released, live performances and doctored versions where I can hear isolated vocals, guitars or a cowbell. Still, that was a pretty good little tape.

No One Will Be Watching Us

I don't get it. I keep hearing all these music folk saying how they prefer the old vinyl records to today's digital formats. "I even miss the scratches and pops," these throwbacks will proclaim, and then will go out and buy up every new album that's still released on vinyl. To me that's like putting spots of strawberry jam all over your face, because you miss the acne of adolescence. No, I just don't get it.

When I recall the limitations of vinyl I most often think of the Beatles' "White Album," as it is commonly called. (The actual name of the record is *The Beatles*.) As a kid I played this album to death, and often said that if I had to take only one album to a deserted island it would be this one. That was cheating, of course, since it was a double-disc album.

It wasn't from excessive play that on my copy the opening piano part to "Martha My Dear" was scratched, and therefore skipped. It was damaged early. In fact, it might even come like that. For years whenever I played the song in my head I always heard the skipping version, and it wasn't until much later, with the arrival of the compact disc, that I finally could hear the song as it was originally intended.

But here's where the vinyl version of *The Beatles* caused me the most trouble. You see, young softie that I was, I was always partial to McCartney's syrupy ballad, "I Will." Still am. And sometimes I was in the mood to hear *only* that song, not the entire album side.

Sure, nowadays I just have to select a track number and I can hear whatever cut I want, as many times as I want, right from the exact beginning. But back then I would have to gently lift the record player's arm and carefully try to drop the needle right in that wide band that separates the songs. It was a skill that required a laser-like concentration and a delicate hand, and I, as a fifteen year old boy, possessed neither.

And so, more often than not, I'd clumsily drop the needle somewhere near the end of the song before "I Will." And that song was also a McCartney song, called "Why Don't We Do It in the Road?" Which usually was no problem; I liked that song too.

The album was released, not coincidentally, about a month before Christmas. And so like millions of kids I had found "The White Album" under the tree that year. And also like millions of kids I wanted to play it as much as I could. Why, I'd even play it right in the middle of a family holiday gathering.

And I swear to you now, when I dropped that needle it wasn't my intent to shock anybody. I just wanted to hear "I Will." In fact, I'll take it a step further and say that I probably wanted *everybody* to hear "I Will." It had been over four years now since I started shilling for those lads from Liverpool.

"Did you hear that? Did you hear what they said?" This came from a very excited Aunt Sylvia. Up until this point I couldn't be sure if anybody was listening to the songs I was playing, but now I knew at least one person was. And that person was Aunt Sylvia. Despite my best efforts she had heard McCartney screeching about doing it in the road, and she was shocked. This was, after all, 1968.

It's sad to think that Aunt Sylvia, a cheery and fun-loving woman, is no longer with us. Still, I can't help but wonder what her reaction would have been if she had heard the lyrics in, say, the rap music of today. I suspect she might have decided that the concept of "doing it in the road" was, after all, rather quaint.

Leonard Stegmann

Cigs

❦❦❦❦❦

I don't know why the price shocked me, but it did. Somewhere along the way when I hadn't been paying attention the price had gone up to fifty, sixty, even seventy dollars, depending on the brand. I couldn't believe it.

"Is that how much a carton of cigarettes costs?" I asked the clerk behind the counter.

"No, we just hang those prices up there as a joke," she was kind enough not to say.

And at this point I'm going to resist taking that high and mighty route that I find so annoying in others. I'm not going to say, Well, I wouldn't know the cost, since I don't smoke and never did. Why, saying something as superior sounding as that would put me right in the same category as those snobs who brag, Oh, I don't even *own* a television. Well, your loss, asshole.

Side Note: Many years ago I had a friend who often bragged that she never watched television. One day we were discussing our favorite writers and she said one of hers was Henry Blake.

"You mean *William* Blake," I corrected. "Henry Blake is on *MASH.*" It was satisfying back then, and, if I'm honest, it still sort of is today.

Several days after I found out the cost of a carton of cigarettes I received an e-mail from a childhood friend. I hadn't heard from her for years, and so when she was bringing me up to date she mentioned that she and her husband were taking care of an old aunt.

"She smokes two cartons of cigarettes a week, at $120 a carton," she wrote.

Now having just learned the cost of cigarettes I thought she must be mistaken, or prone to exaggeration. It was only when researching the cost of a pack of cigarettes that I learned that the price varies a great deal from state to state. New York, where my friend and her aunt live, has one of the highest cigarette taxes in the country. And so $120 for a carton of cigarettes is certainly not out of the question. Which means, and here again I find myself shocked, that the amount the old lady spends on cigarettes in a month is higher than my mortgage payment. Whoa.

Now I doubt that the clerk mentioned above had any interest at all in hearing about the way things used to be in the olden days, but you do, right? Sure you do. And so imagine a very young Leonard riding his bicycle up to Herman's Deli to buy a pack of cigarettes for his mom. I remember doing this many times, and I also remember the price: twenty-six cents a pack. And yes, Herman would sell that pack to a ten year old kid, *if* he happened to have a note from his mother. It was a different time.

And so once again to the inflation calculator, where we find that twenty-six cents in 1963 is the rough equivalent of $1.95 today. Ah, but haven't we just learned that a pack of cigarettes now costs anywhere from five to twelve dollars? My, they really *are* expensive, and I was right to be shocked. Luckily, I don't smoke and never did. I do watch television, though.

That Won't Do You Any Good

Five Whole Dollars

I just read this story about an 83 year old man in Salt Lake City who was so "wracked with guilt" that he returned to the restaurant where he had skipped out on a meal when he was ten to make amends. And so what did he do? Well, the original meal had cost a dollar, but he gave the restaurant five bucks, to pay for the meal and seven decades of interest. Such a heartwarming story, isn't it?

Like hell it is, and here's why. Look, let's not crawl over each other in a rush to shake this geezer's hand for his honesty. Where's the congratulatory pat on the back for those of us who *never* dashed out on a meal, who never shoplifted, who never stole anything except perhaps a young maiden's heart? Nowhere, that's where.

And even forgetting about the morality of this admittedly minor crime committed by a ten year old boy, let's take a good hard look at the mathematics. First of all, the old coot ripped off that restaurant in 1941, basically stealing a 1941 dollar. And yet when it comes time to make his reparations what does he do? He repays the restaurant with a modern-day dollar.

Now a quick trip to my handy inflation calculator tells me that a dollar in 1941 was the equivalent of $15.61 today! Whoa, nice deal you cut for yourself there, Grandpa!

And don't confuse inflation with interest. The owner of this restaurant who had money stolen might very well have invested that dollar in the stock market, which has averaged roughly a ten percent annual return over the last seventy-plus years. Do you know how much that restaurant owner's dollar would have grown to today? $1,051.15! But it didn't…because that young punk stole it.

So there you have it. If that old man truly wanted to make amends he would have given that restaurant $1066.76, to cover both inflation and seventy-three years of interest. (And don't even get me started on punitive damages for pain and suffering.) But no, he gave them five measly dollars. This is not some noble act of restitution, people, it's just some codger trying to buy his way into Heaven, and as cheaply as possible. Well, I got news for you, Pops. God, too, has a calculator. And he knows how to use it.

That Won't Do You Any Good

At the Military Museum

I still can't imagine how my dad, who lived for twenty-five years in his home in Florida, and who could tell you if--and at what time--a flamingo sneezed two counties away, never knew about the military museum just a few miles away. And yet I never heard him mention it, and now it was too late to ask him if he'd ever been there.

I myself had found it out of necessity. Dad had left some, let's call them collectibles, from his time in World War II, and now I needed to figure out what to do with them. His most prized souvenir was a large metal swastika that had once adorned the top of a Nazi flagpole. All the other guys wanted the flags, he had once told me, but I cut off the flag topper. And cut off it had been. The wooden top of the pole was still embedded in the base of the shiny emblem, and I was just a bit stunned when I realized the piece of pole might well have been there since it had been screwed on by another young soldier, this one in a German uniform, over seventy years ago.

There were other bits of memorabilia. There was a dagger as well as a single dinner fork, each emblazoned with a swastika. And there were several albums of photographs, mostly of soldiers relaxing, playing baseball and seeming to be having a fine time. Until you realize that these were the only times that a soldier might be able to take a picture. It was not likely that I'd find a photo taken by a soldier during an actual battle.

And so I drove to the military museum with Dad's treasures. I told myself that it was better to give these items to the museum, where thousands of people could view them, rather than keep them in a closet or drawer, as they had been since about 1946. The deeper truth, of course, is that, while I have always been fascinated with objects from earlier times, I had little to no interest in those involving the military. And so why not donate them to people who did?

The military museum turned out to be a bigger deal than I had expected, leaving me even more befuddled as to how Dad had never discovered it. Despite its size (the hostess at the door would tell me that the museum covered over 30,000 feet) I had to drive around a little to find an available parking space. You see, a large part of the parking lot was taken up by what the sign said was a Russian MiG fighter jet. There were also other quite large military vehicles resting in the nearby grassy area, including an actual tank.

I walked into the front door of the museum and was greeted by a chubby, pretty and quite young girl at the front counter. I told her I had called earlier, and wanted to make a donation. She handed me a form and I began to list the items I had brought. As I did, I asked the girl if they put up a little card of some kind, naming my Dad as the donor. He would have loved that, but no, they didn't do that sort of thing.

As I spoke to the young woman I couldn't help but sneak some peeks over her shoulder, noting what appeared to be a rather vast and extensive series of exhibits inside. And that was just the tiny portion I could see.

"Wow, this place is huge," I said. It was then she told me about the aforementioned square footage. My comment that it was bigger than the Winchester Mystery House was met with a blank stare, and really, why wouldn't it be? The girl was barely out of high school and three thousand miles from California. And so I dropped another hint.

"Looks like you have quite a collection in there," I said, craning my neck in an obvious way.

By now you may have picked up on the fact that I trying to get into the museum for free. Yes, I have little interest in military history and yes, the admission price hovered dangerously close to twenty dollars, but it appeared to be an excellent museum, and I was admittedly curious. Perhaps it's sexist, perhaps it's ageist, but I truly believe that if there had been a man at that front counter, and especially if it had been an older man, I would have heard the words I was trying to coerce out of this young girl: "Go in and have a look around."

I never heard those words, of course, and if you had told me before I arrived I wouldn't be offered a free ticket after I had so generously given them this box of priceless World War II artifacts, I wouldn't have believed it. Things looked different now. The museum was huge, it was surrounded by vintage vehicles and tanks, and there was a fucking fighter plane parked in the driveway. Suddenly Dad's flag-topper and Nazi fork didn't seem quite so impressive.

I handed the form to the girl, who informed me I'd be getting a notice in the mail with the determined value of my donation. For tax purposes, you know. Then, after one last glance into the museum, I thanked the girl and headed towards my car. I started it up and backed up very slowly and carefully. I sure as hell didn't want to smash into that MiG fighter that was parked just a few feet away.

Grandpa Leonard Does It Again

I was going to say this happened in the grocery store, but that's not exactly honest. In truth, I was in the food aisle of the dollar store, and she had now crossed my path for the third time. She was young, perhaps in her mid-twenties, and quite attractive. I watched as she reached up for a box of something--I never knew what--on the top shelf, wondering if she would be able to reach it. And if she couldn't I was standing by, ready and able to use my no more than average height to aid this damsel in distress.

At first it looked like she was not going to need my chivalrous assistance, but then three boxes came tumbling down on her. I instinctively reached out to catch them, missed them all, but valiantly bent down to retrieve the boxes. I handed her one and returned the others to the top shelf.

By now the girl, slightly embarrassed, was laughing and apologizing. I laughed along with her, all the while thinking of something clever to say. Make it witty! I commanded myself. What I said was this:

"Boy, you'd never make it on *The Ed Sullivan Show*."

Now, this was a pretty good line and I'll explain why, because some of you younger men need to hear this. The natural instinct for many men is to rush in, filled with faux concern. Are you alright? they'll fawn, even though she obviously is fine. Or they'll move right in with a compliment. A pretty girl like you should have someone getting those things for you, or some such drivel.

My line was good because, and it would do you young fellows well to remember this, instead of gushing with compliments she was no doubt used to, and perhaps weary of, I gently teased her. I implied that she was clumsy. It's a good approach, and in addition the comment itself was pretty slick for the spur of the moment.

Now, this is why it was a good line but not a *great* line, and I suspect you've already figured this out. Two seconds after I spoke I wanted to take back my words and do some quick editing. As mildly clever as my line was, I couldn't help but sense that this fresh, young girl, decades my junior, was now thinking, Who the fuck is Ed Sullivan?

You see, it *would* have been a great line if this incident had taken place in, say, 1967, but sadly it did not. I later tortured myself by recognizing what a simple matter it would have been to replace *The Ed Sullivan Show* with perhaps a program that hadn't been off the air since

Nixon's first term. I could have said, Boy, you'd never make it on *America's Got Talent*, or even, I wouldn't want to see that on YouTube. But no, I had to mention a guy who had already been long dead before she was even born.

Ah well, I thought, driving away consuming my dollar store Diet Coke and peanut butter-filled pretzels. I suppose it could have been even worse. I might have said, Boy, you'd never make it on Major Bowes.

One of these days I really must update my references.

Leonard Stegmann

Eighteen Cents

"Do you want your eighteen cents?"

I wasn't sure I had heard correctly, so I asked her to repeat it. And so she did, and my suspicion was confirmed: the girl behind the counter had just asked me, in essence, if I wanted my change from the sandwich I had just purchased.

I didn't get all huffy or nasty, although I might plead guilty to displaying a mild indignation. It was, after all, only eighteen cents. Still, in my many years of walking this foul planet I don't ever recall being asked a question like that. Of *course* I wanted my eighteen cents, and now, having been asked this odd and possibly offensive question, even more so.

Specifically, her actual response, when asked to repeat it, had been, "Do you want your eighteen cents? Most people don't." I doubted that very much. Sure, when asked, some of the weaker-willed people probably said, "Nah, keep it." But it is very unlikely that they were in the majority, and they certainly weren't me.

And so I wondered if the repeatedly pierced, heavily tattooed but not unattractive girl behind the counter had a nice little side business going. Eighteen cents here, forty-nine cents there and you might end up with a nice little bonus by the end of each day. Well, sorry Honey, but your daily take is going to be a little short today. A dime, a nickel and three pennies short, to be precise.

The girl handed me my change, I thanked her and stood there with the coins in my hand, not really sure what to do next. Where, I wondered, am I supposed to put these coins? Oh, I forget to mention one little fact: At the time this transaction occurred I was naked. I had ordered my BLT at the snack bar in a nudist community, and now stood in the air-conditioned room with my sandwich in one hand and five coins in the other.

And sure, I had seen the tip jar from the moment I walked in, but I sure wasn't about to put my eighteen cents in there now. I do have my pride, despite the image of myself I've just created in your head. And so I walked towards the door, struggled to open it, having no free hands, and made my way into the oppressive Florida heat, where I proceeded to eat my sandwich, after having first spread my eighteen cents on the table in front of me.

Hey, it's nice when someone leaves you a tip for good service. In some places it's even required. But asking a man if he wants his change? I'm sorry, but this simply isn't done. No, not even if that man is naked.

Leonard Stegmann

Mellow Yellow

You might be too young to remember this, but there was a time in this country when people believed that you could get high from smoking a banana. This was in the late 1960's, and I might have been one of those people.

Oh hell, we all were. The rumor was that you could get high from a banana. Now, the first impression for many of us was putting a banana in your mouth and lighting the other end. Then more "information" became available. The trick was to scrape the inside of the banana, and then dry the material in the oven until it turned into a black powder. You could then smoke this powder, which was called bananadine, and get high after three or four cigarettes.

Right now I have no doubt that there are still thousands of aging hippies out there who, although they won't admit it, actually tried this. I'm happy to say that I never did, although the reasons were probably because I was only in my early teens and so still living at home. I couldn't begin to imagine my parents' reaction if they had walked into the kitchen and seen me cooking banana scrapings.

The rumor, I remember, swept through the country like wildfire. I even recall Bob Hope dressed as a hippie on one of his specials and waving around a banana like a cigar. He had a funny line, too, but I'm afraid that quip is lost to the ages.

It was years later, long after I, and just about everybody else, had stopped thinking about it that I first heard that the idea of getting high from smoking a banana had been a hoax. It was started in the March, 1967 of the *Berkeley Barb*. I know what you're thinking. *Berkeley?* No way!

The idea was to see how the government would react if something as common as a banana was found to contain a psychoactive ingredient. Would they be forced to stay consistent in their drug policy, and therefore make bananas illegal? Researchers soon found out that there was no chemical that could make you high, and any effect that was felt was of the placebo variety.

Today we laugh that people could be so gullible. The idea of getting high from a banana is just too ridiculous for words. Now, snorting grape Kool-Aid, that's another story.

Leonard Stegmann

Unconsumed Ice Cream, and Other Myths

It was, to me anyway, an extraordinary phenomenon on par with sightings of Big Foot and alien abductions where they stick hoopdejoobs up your most personal of parts. It was so rare an occurrence, in fact, that I still remember when I witnessed it, even though it was a long time ago: It was the first week of August, 1981.

Leonard, what *are* you talking about? Well, I'll tell you. First, a little background. I have here on my desk a scrap of paper from a magazine I was recently reading in the, oh, let's say den. I believe it is from an article in *National Geographic*, an article that, sadly, I didn't bother to read, or scan with enough depth to even know what it was about. Along with the article, however, was this chart, and that is what I tore from the *NatGeo* and placed on my desk.

Clearly, we can assume that the story that I didn't bother to read concerned itself in some way with all the food that is wasted in this country. I come to this conclusion because the chart is topped with some statistics giving the cost of all the food that is left unconsumed in the United States. Wasted food, it seems, is responsible for 2.5% of our energy consumption, more than 25% of the fresh water used in agriculture, 300 million barrels of oil and the loss of $115 billion a year.

Yeah, yeah, yeah, but here's where it gets interesting. The chart does a comparison of certain types of food, and the percentage of each that goes to waste. F'rinstance, since hard cheeses last much longer than their softer cousins, only 8% of Parmesan cheese goes to waste, as opposed to a full 50% of Swiss. Pumpkins, as we know, are used mostly for carving, so a whopping 69% of them are not eaten but simply thrown away each year. And each year Americans spend about $900 million on tomatoes that they never eat!

But that's not the most shocking bit of information to be found in this chart, at least to me it isn't. And this is where you came in. It was August of 1981 and I had just moved to the Bay Area. I was staying with some friends and happened to be exploring the contents of their refrigerator one lonely and hungry night. I looked in the freezer and there I saw it. It was a sight I still remember to this day, and am not likely to *ever* forget.

True, it was some years ago, and so you'll forgive me if I don't recall the brand, or even the flavor. I was, in fact, quite excited when I first discovered it; an excitement that immediately turned to horror once I had managed to pry open the circular lid. It was a half-gallon of ice cream, or at least it had once been. What I was looking at now was dry, hardened and like nothing I had ever before seen.

Yes, it was some ice cream that had been there long enough to go bad! And although I was already a grown man at this point, this was something I had never before seen or, to be honest, even contemplated. How could you have ice cream in the house and not eat it? I mean, if not the first night then surely within the next day or so? I think I once had a pint of Ben and Jerry's that lasted for over 72 hours, but that was only because I had contracted a violent stomach flu, and for once had more things coming out of my body than going in.

But there it had been, covered in ice crystals and stashed way in the rear of the freezer. It was indeed ice cream that actually needed to be thrown out. Which I didn't do, of course. With a shiver of disgust I put the lid back on the container and closed the freezer door. Believe me when I tell you I didn't sleep well that night.

According to the chart provided by the good folks at *National Geographic*, a full 24% of ice cream will face the same fate as that horribly deformed half-gallon I stumbled upon all those decades ago. Someone will buy some ice cream, perhaps eat a bit and then either forget about the rest of it or, inconceivably, just not want it.

Listen, *National Geographic* is a distinguished magazine with a long, honorable history, and if they say something, it is no doubt true. And so if they tell me that nearly a quarter of all the ice cream purchased in the United States ends up getting thrown out, well, I believe it without hesitation. I'll just never understand it.

Leonard Stegmann

The Garage Door and the Toilet Seat

Now I was scared. We were just about ready to sign on the dotted line, when our real estate agent decided that there was no way her clients are going to buy a house with a garage door in *that* condition. "We aren't?" I thought to myself.

And so the deal was put on hold, and I sweated thinking that our agent had blown our only chance of owning this tiny beach house on the *good* side of Highway One. I needn't have worried. A short time later, in lieu of adjusting all the completed paperwork, we received a check for $700 to replace the crumbling garage door.

And replace it we did, a mere eleven years later. Well, you know, I've been busy. I told a friend this story and he said it was a good thing we had saved that money all these years. And then we both laughed loudly.

"Garage doors cost a lot more than that now," our neighbor warned more than once during our conversation. She then handed me the slip of paper on which she had written the name and telephone number of her "garage door guy." His name was Arthur. And I would call him, but I learned a long time ago the value of a second opinion, at least when it comes to home repairs. (With doctors, on the other hand, who can be bothered?)

The first man who came out gave the rotting garage door his profession look-see and then said it would cost $1300 to replace. "Ouch!" I thought, which is no surprise, as this would have been my reaction to any amount over, say, twenty bucks. I thanked him for his time and told him I'd be in touch. Then I called Arthur.

Arthur looked at the garage door, asked a few questions and then wrote a number down on his order form: $750. I smiled knowingly, and asked him what the total would be, with installation and tax. "That *is* the total," he said. Glory be.

I signed the order form faster than just about anything I've signed in my life. The garage door, along with Arthur, arrived a few weeks later and was installed. The generic almond color was a near perfect complement to our house, and even the neighbor across the street said our new garage door looked great. That's the kind of thing that neighbors say to each other. When they're not talking about the weather.

And so now we were in the spirit. I can't say for sure that our toilet seat was as old as the garage door had been, but it was fast approaching a similar state of disrepair. Finally, one of the hinges snapped, so I know that when a visiting old girlfriend used the bathroom last week she had gotten much more of a ride than she had expected. (Just like she used to with me. Ahem.)

With Spike at work the purchasing of the new toilet seat was in my hands. "Don't get white," said Spike. "They show everything." Well yes, and yuck, but isn't that why we occasionally *clean* them? And so off to the hardware store I went.

I was surprised, and frankly glad, to find a selection that was not particularly huge. The prices varied, but not by a lot; mostly in the $20 - $30 range. Curiously, the colors didn't offer much of a range, either. Basically there was white and there was cream. Or almond, or beige or sand or whatever the hell they call it. And since Spike had specifically said not to get white, the choice was easy. I got not-white.

I did get caught up, though, just for a minute. One of the toilet seats was one of those "soft" ones, but that's not what attracted me to it. No, it was the colorful little sailboats stitched into the lid. How cute! And how perfect for a beach toilet! I even went so far as carrying the thing a few steps, but then I stopped.

Somewhere in my memory, and I don't know from when, I have an oh-so-faint recollection of once having owned a soft toilet seat. And while I couldn't remember the precise experience, I had a vague but very real feeling that it wasn't a good one. It may have had something to do with the plastic cracking rather quickly, and the resulting edges pinching my delicate heinie. I got the hard seat instead.

Once home, I immersed myself in the task of installing the toilet seat. (I had already removed the old seat before leaving the house. I suppose I hadn't much thought about what I might do if the hardware store didn't happen to carry toilet seats.) Now, many of you know about my experiences with installing things (I still sometimes wake up in a cold sweat after dreaming about the bathroom sink fiasco) but this was a toilet seat, not a garage door, for God's sake. Two plastic bolts, that's all it took.

And yet I couldn't get it to work. Sure, I bolted both hinges of the seat just fine, but I couldn't get the little plastic triangular covers (you had to be there) to snap on. They just didn't fit. What's wrong with this toilet seat? Is there a manufacturer's defect? Do I have to take the damn thing back?

And then I did something that I loathe to do with every fiber of my being, something that goes against everything I stand for: I read the directions. Oh, I see. On this particular "model" you just screw the bolt to the toilet. Then the toilet seat attaches to the bolts with a twist of these handy bits. My, that's a new way of doing it. Is it an improvement? Not likely.

No matter, a bolt here and a twist there and the new toilet seat is securely in place, where it is likely to remain for a long, long time. Probably until the next person who owns this place feels a hinge snap beneath him. Maybe he'll replace the garage door at the same time.

That Won't Do You Any Good

Kick the Can

I watched a particularly poignant episode of *The Twilight Zone* over the weekend. It was about a group of people who lived in an old-age home, or whatever the acceptable term is these days. A bunch of kids were playing outside the home, upsetting some of the residents while causing feelings of nostalgia in others.

The game the kids were playing was also the title of the episode, which was "Kick the Can." Several of the old folks were reminded of the times in their youth when they, too, had spent seemingly endless days playing this game. Watching the game on TV brought back some childhood memories for me as well, memories that, while not negative in any way, were also not particularly warm and nostalgic.

I was fortunate enough to grow up on a street where there were a lot of neighborhood kids running around, and we often played organized games in various sized group. Some of the more popular games were baseball, kickball and hide-and-go-seek. On more than one occasion the grown-ups (old men in their thirties and forties) on the block attempted to introduce us to kick the can. You could tell that they had enjoyed playing the game as kids, and thought it would be fun for us, the next generation, as well.

But we kids didn't think it was much fun at all, and I'm really at a loss to explain why. Sure, we tried to play the game a couple of times but, for whatever reason, it just never caught on. In fact, as soon as the grown-ups went back inside to ease themselves into their overstuffed couches, we'd immediately revert back to one of our regular games.

I was fairly certain I remembered how the game is played, but I just looked it up anyway. It turns out I was pretty close, which you'll agree is not bad for someone who last played the game over fifty years ago, and only twice at that. Basically, a can is set up in an open area, and one person is designated as "It." (That term probably wouldn't fly today, as it would be considered too detrimental to the poor child's self-esteem. He'd probably have to be called "The King," or something equally ego-boosting.)

Next, all the players try to get close enough to the can to kick it (obviously) before they are tagged by It. There are many variations of the game, which I certainly don't feel like going into right now. If you're that curious you can always look it up yourself. There's this thing called the Internet.

Why kick the can, so popular with kids in the 1930's and 1940's and before, would lay such an egg in the

1960's is anybody's guess. Sure, that previous generation was growing up in a depression, and so maybe an old dented can was all the sports equipment they could come up with, but I don't think that's the reason.

We certainly didn't grow up in poverty, but most of our games, such as kickball and curb-ball, could be played with nothing but a single ball. And hide-and-seek required no equipment at all. Nope, I have no idea why we never took to the game kick the can, as had generations of children before us. We just didn't like it.

Leonard Stegmann

I Found a Dollar

༺༺༺༺༺༺

Is there anything quite so beautiful as looking on the ground and seeing money lying there? And I'm not talking about your nearly-worthless nickel, dime or quarter here. I mean good old folding money, the green stuff. It looks so out of place lying there, and seems to radiate with real value, making all the surrounding crap on the street look even, well, crappier.

It's funny what goes through your mind at times like these. Your first thought is not, Oh, goody, a buck. Now I can go to Starbucks and buy a quarter of a cup of coffee!

No, your first thought, before you even determine the denomination, is Cash! There's cash there. And it might be more than one bill. It might be a folded stack! And then, if it happens to be just a dollar, you calm down and mask your disappointment. But that doesn't stop you from swooping down on it like an eagle on an unlucky salmon.

I was walking along the sidewalk the other day, minding my own business (for the time being, anyway) when I looked down and saw it. It was a dollar bill. I did my swooping and then immediately looked around for some more. There wasn't any. The bill was soggy from a recent rain and so I put it in my pocket, so as not to affect the other, drier, bills in my wallet.

And then I laughed. You see I haven't yet grown so old and bitter (check back in a few months) that I still can't find the humor in finding a dollar bill right in front of the dollar store. Well, I thought, at least one of my items today would be free.

My next thought was to give the dollar to the old lady who sits in front of the dollar store all day long, collecting for some charity. That seemed like a good idea, and so I walked towards her and her little table with the coffee can on it.

Then I got close enough to get a good look at that coffee can. The first thing I saw was a cross. Clearly this was some kind of religious charity, so strike one. Actually, to be honest, it was strike three. And then I read the words that said, "Help Keep Kids Off Drugs." Strike four.

I mean, when I was a kid, was there anybody there to help keep me off drugs? No there wasn't, and I am thankful every single day for it. I had a lot of fun on drugs, kept it within reason, and then outgrew it. So who am I to deprive a child of that same enjoyment? Why, it would be the height of hypocrisy at the very least, not to mention outrageously selfish. And so I walked past the old lady and into the dollar store.

I bought six or seven things, but did not use the soggy dollar in my jeans. When I got home I put the dollar on the dresser and it was dry the next day. I put it into my wallet. And no, I can't tell you what I bought with it. Why would I even pay attention to that? It's a just a dollar. And besides, I do have several others in my wallet, you know.

That Won't Do You Any Good

I Could Care Less

This one began, as so many earth-shaking occurrences do, on the pages of Facebook. That's sarcasm, Folks. Learn to recognize and understand it, because it plays an important part in tonight's tirade.

I had posted one of my typically snarky comments about how thrilled I was about the birth of the new royal over in England, saying it was nice to know that even at this advanced age there are still brand new events occurring about which I couldn't care less.

And that's exactly the phrase I used: "Couldn't care less." And I used it consciously, knowing that if I had instead selected the words I actually preferred, "could care less," some pain in the ass would have pointed out, incorrectly, that that meant I *did* care, at least to some degree. Someone saying "I could care less" when one means "I couldn't care less" has become the pet peeve of many people. And they're all idiots.

And sure as hell, two comments later some chick, offended that some of us couldn't appreciate the nearly-divine importance of the royal birth, was commenting on this very topic, criticizing the use of "I could care less." I quickly checked my post again, worried that I had used "could" by mistake. But I hadn't. The critique, it turned out, was directed at the person who had made a comment after mine. Thank God. I really wasn't in the mood.

The two expressions mean almost exactly the same thing. When you say "I couldn't care less," you are being literal. When you say "I could care less," you are being sarcastic. For example, have you ever said, "I just *love* going to the dentist"? Did you mean it? Well, maybe a few of you sick twists did, but for most of you it was sarcasm. Or maybe that's a poor example. I mean, that woman who thought the royal birth was so exciting was, after all, British. What do they know about dentists?

I even did a little research on this today. There was actually a bit of debate about it among some linguists. I forget who or when exactly, and I'm much too lazy to look it up again, but one major league linguist pointed out that the phrase using "could" was sarcasm, and therefore just as valid as using "couldn't." Another camp said that using "could" was incorrect and the result of people dropping the "n't" at the end of the word due to laziness.

Which was the dumbest thing I'd heard all day. Except for, of course, all the news coverage about the birth of the royal brat. How many words can you think of that are used incorrectly, to actually mean the opposite of what was intended, because people were too lazy to finish saying them completely? Exactly.

Well, that's our lesson for today. I hope you learned a little something. And if nothing else, I'm sure that you all found this look at our English language so *very* interesting.

Leonard Stegmann

La Propina

൶൶൶൶൶

"That's too much," said Spike.
"No, it isn't," I countered.
"That's thirty percent," she persisted.
"It's between fifteen and twenty percent," I responded.
"You're supposed to calculate the tip based on the amount *before* the tax," she expounded.
"I taught you that," I retorted.
"There's that 17% tax here in Mexico," she pointed out.
"Well, I don't see it on the bill," I observed.
"Why isn't it there?" she inquired.
"How the hell should I know?" I rejoined.
"I can come back," said the waitress.

I told the waitress that it wouldn't be necessary and we left the pile of pesos on the table for her. Back in the room I found a pen and a piece of paper and, for the first time in perhaps forty years, I did long division. When I was done (admittedly some time later) I showed the result to Spike. We had left approximately an 18.2% tip; a nice amount to be sure, but certainly nobody but the most parsimonious of tightwads would consider it excessive.

Spike tried to continue supporting her weak-ass argument by bringing up the 17% tax we had paid on all other meals in Mexico, but I put an end to that by showing her the bill. The tax, for whatever reason, simply wasn't there. Having proven my point I could have simply leaned back, digested the delicious meal and basked in the afterglow of once again having been right. Yes, I could have.

"You know, the supposed extra amount you didn't want to leave was the equivalent of about forty-eight cents. Twenty-four cents each," I said.

"That's not the point. I didn't want to leave a 30% tip," she said.
"It wasn't. It was 18.2%"
"That's after the 17% tax had been added,"
"There was no 17% tax,"
"Why not?"
"Who's on first?"
"What?"
"Never mind. You're right. That waitress is probably just going to waste that forty-eight cents on silly things, like food and clothing for her family."
"Good night."
"Good night."

Leonard Stegmann

Where Am I?

~~~~~~

Two hundred books. That's what I had collected in the cluster of cardboard boxes that were scattered around my living room floor. Two hundred books weeded from just two bookshelves. (And the surrounding floor.) And the bookshelves were still filled with more.

Each year a local church holds a book sale and I look forward to it like a kid to Christmas. About three months ago I decided I'd give back, and donate books that I would never read, or never read again. I did it out of the kindness of my heart, to clear my nearly-buried bookshelves and, of course, for the inflated tax deduction.

Included in these books I had found several copies of my own first two books, and decided what the hell. I'll include them in the donation and who knows where they might end up. I mean, besides the most likely fate of rotting for years in the moldy church basement.

And now this weekend it was finally once again time for the book fair, and so I made my way to the church parking lot carrying a black book bag with the AAA logo on it. Hey, it was free. I was there, as usual, to fill that bag and begin the process of once again burying my still-straining bookshelves.

I also was interested to find out where my own books had ended up, and maybe, just maybe, catch some bargain hunter flipping through, or even buying, one of them. I suppose I also wanted to make sure the books had been placed in the proper section. Like me, they're exquisite gems that are not easily categorized.

F'rintstance, on more than one occasion I've walked into the local bookstore to find my book *A Year on Planet Mercury* jammed onto the geek-filled science fiction shelf. Sure, the title is somewhat misleading, and the cover shows a lady lying down on the surface of a desolate planet, presumably Mercury, but Jesus, make an effort and crack open the cover and at least read the table of contents, will you?

I began, as I usually do, by looking at the huge selection of hardcover fiction books filling the boxes that lined the sidewalk. I was chiefly looking for something to read, of course, but still kept an eye open for my books. I wouldn't have been surprised if one of them had been dumped into a fiction box by a harried church lady, but a half hour, and hundreds of titles, later I realized that it hadn't.

My next stop was the Humor section. This, I felt, is where I belonged. (Despite the none-too-subtle critiques of so many, many people.) There was just a small box for Humor, and it included exactly who I expected to find there, including David Sedaris and Dave Barry, as well as four near-antique paperback joke books that I immediately recognized, since a few months earlier they had been squeezed into a corner of my very own bookshelf. The only thing that seemed to be missing from the Humor box was, well, me.

A short time later I found myself looking through the History and Politics section. Here I found some modern-day humorists, including Michael Moore and Jon Stewart. (And all your other liberal friends, my dad might say.) And it might be a stretch to say I write about history and politics, but who else has taken more cheap shots at George W. or written so extensively (and passionately) about the history of the brassiere? Exactly.

Nope, I wasn't in this box either. Nor, as the morning turned into afternoon, did I find a single copy of my books in the Gardening, Religion, Coffee Table, Travel or Children's sections, or thrown into the disorganized pile of archaic VHS tapes that was melting in the noon sun.

So what was the story here? I wondered. I had donated about five or six copies of my books. Where were they? Had they not been put out for sale? Had they been rejected by the folks who ran the church? Had it come

That Won't Do You Any Good

to this: that I couldn't even *give away* copies of my books?

I took a few deep breaths and tried to be rational about the situation. Of course some of the books were my very first one, the unfortunately named *Heywood Jablomi*; a title so embarrassingly juvenile that I couldn't even answer women if they asked me the title of my only book. "It's, uh, humor," I'd stammer more often than not.

So perhaps the church fathers had gathered up the three or four copies of *Heywood* that I had donated and had had a small, but vengeful, bonfire last night behind the rectory. (Do Lutheran churches have rectories? And why does that word sound obscene?) I immediately dismissed the bonfire idea. It was unlikely that any of these fine Christians would have picked up on the foul name of the book; or repeated it to anyone if they had.

And I eventually came to the only conceivable explanation for the absence of my books. It was so obvious that my legion of readers had arrived at the sale the minute it opened, and scoured each and every box for the rare, and hugely underpriced, copies of my books. There could be no other logical reason for the current dearth of my books.

My God, I thought, there must have been fights breaking out all over the parking lot, as dozens of my fans scratched and clawed for the too few literary treasures that bore my name. I'm glad I had come later in the day, or the situation might have become even more grievous.

I was just about to leave when I looked into one more box, and there, at long last, I saw several copies, three or four, of my books. So they hadn't been burned in a fire by religious fanatics after all, nor had they been snatched up by a rabid gang of my fans. (Not *all* of them, anyway. Ahem.)

I quickly looked up to the handwritten sign over the table to see exactly which category my books had been assigned. And I saw one single word, written in magic marker on an old piece of cardboard nailed to a stick. And that word was: Classics. And so there I was, nestled in comfortably with the likes of Nathaniel Hawthorne, Herman Melville, Louisa May Alcott and William Shakespeare.

"Well, of course," I laughed to myself. Where else *would* I be?

That Won't Do You Any Good

Mid-Island Memories

The problem was I had really wanted to see *and* hear this movie, but the latter had become impossible because of all the screaming girls. No, it wasn't the latest terrifying horror film that had loosed this feminine teenaged cacophony; it was the Beatles' movie *A Hard Day's Night*.

After the film my friends and I ran home, frequently looking back over our shoulders to see if any girls were gaining on us. We were lost in the fantasy, despite our pre-teen age, short hair and total lack of any musical ability whatsoever, that we were indeed the Beatles. As I grew older I came to accept that I was not one of the Beatles, and never would be, a reality I would always regard as a horrible, and almost unspeakably cruel, trick of fate.

I remembered this day when the theater itself came up in a conversation today. It was the Mid-Island movie theater, and it was one of two in our town. Frankly, when it comes to fond movie theater memories, it was that *other* theater that mists these old eyes. It was there that I could buy a ticket for a quarter, and candy for a nickel. And it was there that I spent many happy hours sitting in the dark enjoying such Saturday afternoon mainstays as *The House on Haunted Hill, Gorgo* and *The Creature From the Black Lagoon.*

And then one day they built the Mid-Island. Unlike the other theater, which was, in all honesty, something of a dump, and may not have actually been built as a movie theater at all, The Mid-Island was a slick, modern glass-and-brick affair that was nothing short of cutting edge in 1961. It had its drawbacks, of course, chief among them was that they charged *thirty*-five cents to get in.

The Mid-Island had a loge, a section of seats that were isolated from us riff-raff by aluminum railings. I never did sit in that section, but shocked myself often by touching the railings after having shuffled across the thick carpet. The Mid-Island also had loveseats, so that a romantic young couple could sit close and snuggle as they watched the movie. I never did sit in a loveseat, either. By the time I was old enough to, uh, snuggle, I no longer went to the Mid-Island. And doing so now at this point, at any theater, seems like it would just be uncomfortable and annoying.

The most frightened I have ever been by a movie happened at the Mid-Island. The film was *Premature Burial.* It was based on the Poe story and told the tale of a man being buried alive, and he was helpless to do anything about it. One scene showed the burial of the coffin, which for some reason had a handy window, from the victim's point of view. "I'm alive! Oh, why can't they hear me?" he moaned as he was lowered into the grave. That fucking movie scared the beejeebers out of me.

Once, when I was about thirteen, and not a petite thirteen either, my father dropped me off at the theater. "Tell them you're eleven," he ordered. Now, even *I* thought that was pushing it, but I did as I was told, asking for the kid's ticket price. The ticket-seller's reaction was a combination of disbelief and disgust. "Ah, c'mon," he said, or something close to it. But I was already committed, so I shakily insisted that I was eleven. I got the kid's ticket and never did anything like that again.

Several years later I was filled with teenage rebellion and ready to fight any injustice that I came across, whether it was actual or not. My friends and I were going to see a movie at the Mid-Island. We knew that they had recently raised their prices, but normally we'd see a double feature. This time we'd be paying their exorbitant price for just a single film.

This was the sixties, and protest was in the air. Message buttons were all the rage, and some of us even had button-making kits. And so before we left for the theater I made a large white button with stark, highly visible black lettering. It read: "$1.25 FOR ONLY ONE MOVIE?" Filled half with self-righteous indignation and half with fear, I marched up to the ticket window, chest thrust out, my badge of rebellion exposed to the world. Nobody noticed.

After today's conversation I searched for a picture of the Mid-Island Theater in its glory days and, surprisingly, came up empty. I did find one photo of the old place. It was taken as the theater was being demolished in 2006. The theater was little more than a ruin by this point. And you know, I'm not really one of those people who shakes his head sadly every time an old structure is torn down.

Sure, there are some buildings, very few, which should be preserved because of their history, but the Mid-Island wasn't one of them. Still, it was a place where I had once, a long time ago, laughed at Jerry Lewis, sang along with the Beatles, gotten turned on by Stella Stevens and been scared out of my mind by Edgar Allan Poe. And most of the time for only thirty-five cents.

That Won't Do You Any Good

The Snack Whore

ଶ୍ୱେଶ୍ୱେଶ୍ୱେ

Mostly it's because of the medicine, but I suppose I should take some of the blame. Celine the cat has been on steroids for a while now, and they've done wonders to improve her condition. Unfortunately the drugs have also spawned a dramatic increase in her appetite.

"For now, just give her food whenever she wants some," advises the doctor.

And by "doctor" I actually mean "veterinarian." And so it got to the point where I was refilling Celine's bowl two, three, even four times a day. This, as expected, has led to a two pound weight gain, which may not sound like a lot, but when you think of it as an overall expansion of 20%, well, how many pounds would you have to pack on to increase your weight by 20%?

Celine has always been something of a snack whore, but it's recently gotten much worse. Every time I'm in the kitchen, where the cat snacks are kept, guess who comes trotting in a short time later? Sometimes I leave her sleeping in the living room, snoring and seemingly out to the world, and thirty seconds later I'm laughing out loud. I didn't see her come in, I didn't hear her bells jingling, but I look down and there she is at my feet, looking up at me with those snack-craving eyes. It's like she's some sort of ghost-cat who can materialize at will from another dimension.

And so of course she gets a snack. Now, at this point I only give her one or two, in an attempt to stretch her daily snack ration over the course of her many visits to the kitchen.

"How many snacks can you eat in one day, kitty cat?" I ask her.

I mean, I wondered how this cat could come into the kitchen every single time I go in in there and consume yet another snack. Is this normal? Is this healthy? Or is it some kind of twisted, compulsive eating disorder?

And then yesterday I had a revelation, hitting me like a lightning bolt from above. Every time Celine followed me into the kitchen because she wanted a snack, *I had gone into the kitchen to get myself a snack.* Whoa. No wonder the cat was giving me the evil eye. Here I was asking her how many times a day she needed a snack, judging her, when all she was doing, in essence, was trying to keep up with me! Boy, I thought, was this ever a clear case of the pot calling the kitty black.

Pillow Talk

I'm not psychic. Nobody is. Still, I just knew it was going to end this way. I was squeezing my way towards the window seat, mentally preparing for the four hour flight from San Salvador to Lima, when I saw them. Not one, but *two* pillows waiting for me on my seat.

It was like some vision out of the not too distant past; a time not so very long ago when you could expect a pillow, blanket, hot towel and even a meal on your flight. I was surprised to learn that those days never actually disappeared, as I had thought. They just no longer existed on the flights of American airline companies.

Well, I already had my inflatable neck cushion, and so I felt that keeping both of these pillows as well might somehow be perceived as…piggy. And so once in my seat I turned to Spike and asked her if she would like one of my pillows.

"No, thank you," she said, and quite clearly. Are you sure? No, she didn't want one.

Well, I still felt something akin to a pillow glutton, and so I turned to the fellow in the seat behind me and held up the extra pillow.

"Would you like this?" I offered.

He never answered, or even smiled, but nodded with a grunt and took the pillow. I must confess, I was a bit chuffed by his less-than-enthusiastic response. Would it have taken so much effort to spit out a thank you, in any language, rather than the guttural sound he emitted? After all, I didn't *have* to offer the thug the pillow. I could have kept them both, and virtually padded my entire body for the flight ahead.

Finally, I reminded myself that I had only handed the guy an anemic little airline pillow, not a pot of gold or the keys to Oz. Still, I thought that had been rather nice of me. And so I settled back to enjoy the flight, comforted by both the pillow I retained and the overwhelming sense of my own wonderfulness.

Okay, now it's your turn to participate. How long do you think it took? Ten Minutes? Half an hour? Wrong! It was no less than sixty seconds after I had donated my extra pillow to that gruff stranger behind me that Spike turned to me and spoke these words:

"You know, I think I *will* take that pillow."

And the thing was, I wasn't the least bit surprised. I knew I could have asked her a dozen or fifty or a google number of times if she wanted it, and she would have said no each and every time. But the second it was gone, and I had only the one pillow…

Oh, maybe I huffed and puffed a bit, and pointed out in my exasperation that I had just asked if she wanted the pillow not more than a minute earlier. But in the end I, of course, gave my one and only pillow to Spike to use on the flight. And so now found, only a short time after being mesmerized by the bounty of pillows I had discovered on my seat, that I had none. Why did I do it? Didn't you read the part where I talked about my overwhelming wonderfulness?

Leonard Stegmann

Spike's New Uncle

෴෴෴෴෴

It was bad news, no doubt about it. We had just listened to a message that had been left by Spike's aunt a few hours earlier. She's well into her eighties and lives several thousand miles away. Spike calls her a few times a year, and almost never sees her. Spike's aunt *never* calls her. That is, until today.

"Somebody died," I said as soon as the message was played. Spike readily agreed. But who? We had already planned on meeting with a few neighbors, and so postponed the phone call until later. On the walk down the street we discussed the morbid possibilities.

"I have a distant relative who lives near her," said Spike. "I bet it's him."

"What about that nice lady who came with your aunt to visit us?" I guessed.

"That's right, her cousin," agreed Spike. "It must be her."

"That's too bad. She was really sweet," I said, already downgrading the poor woman to the past tense.

"Yeah, she was," said Spike, also making the transition rather flawlessly.

"Well, at least you know it's not your aunt." I joked. "Well, actually, she *could* be calling about some bad medical news."

We met up with our neighbors, kept our commitment and about a half hour later we were walking back home.

"I guess I better call my aunt and get it over with," sighed Spike. And so she did.

I sat at this very computer, a short distance away, while Spike talked to her aunt. The conversation started with the usual greetings and small talk. I could only hear one side of the conversation, of course, but it didn't take Columbo to fill in the gaps. Suddenly I could feel the tone of the conversation change, and I knew that Spike's aunt was getting ready to drop the reason why she had called.

"What? You did? When? Uh, congratulations," said Spike.

And that's all it took. I started laughing hysterically from my station at the computer. Nobody was sick. Nobody had died. The big news was that Spike's aunt, just a few months short of her 87th birthday, had gotten married. Boy, we never saw *that* one coming.

Leonard Stegmann

My Short Career at Short

I'm not talking about some hateful thing we once said to a loved one in a time of anger, or that horrible thing we did and wish for the rest of our lives that we could take back. I suspect we all have one or two of those that we carry around with us, tucked way down deep inside.

No, I'm talking about some silly and wildly insignificant episode that perhaps bothered us at the time, but which should have been completely gone from our memory banks by the next morning. But wasn't. And now years later we still cringe every time we think about it, no matter how much we know it shouldn't matter.

Here's mine:

I was playing in a co-ed softball league at the time. It's not the sort of thing I would generally gravitate to, but my girlfriend had insisted, and the truth was it was kind of fun. More fun than that bowling league, anyway.

For whatever reason I showed up late that evening, and the game had already begun. Actually I had rushed straight from work, and had arrived with my head still in corporate mode. As it turned out, being a little late did not make me the most unreliable member of the team that night, as several people hadn't bothered to show up at all. A quick greeting to my girlfriend and other teammates, and then I found out they had been talking about me before I arrived. In fact, they had big plans for me.

"You're going in at short," said Ron, our pitcher and unofficial, and self-appointed, team captain.

Now it was true that I had probably played a lot more baseball in my life than most of the guys (and all of the women) on the team. Not particularly well, mind you, but I knew the game. The truth was, though, I had never played shortstop anywhere. Not on an organized team and not in street games. I weakly made this point, but I knew it was no use. The team, that is to say, Ron, had decided.

It was quite a compliment, really. And so I trotted out to this totally alien location, pounded my glove a couple of times and nodded to Ron that I was ready, let's get this show on the road.

Let me tell you something about Ron. I didn't know Ron before I had joined this league. In fact, I hadn't known anybody on the team, except, of course, my girlfriend. In the beginning I liked Ron. He seemed nice enough, and I thought that I saw the start of, as they said in that old movie, a beautiful friendship.

Now, after a few games, I wasn't so sure. We all wanted to win, but Ron *really* wanted to win. He was not above slamming his mitt on the ground in disgust if someone made a mistake in the field, or even yelling at a teammate if his play didn't live up to Ron's expectations. Did I mention that this was a slow-pitch, co-ed softball league?

The first batter up hit a clean single to right field, putting him, of course, on first base.

"Play is to second," Ron said to me, as if I hadn't been playing baseball all my life. It didn't matter because the next batter hit a double right up the middle, scoring the runner. Clearly this wasn't going well, and Ron was starting to fume.

With a runner on second, the next batter hit a not-too sharp grounder right at me, the first time I had touched the ball as a shortstop in my life. I scooped up the ball cleanly, despite the runner rushing by me to third, and mentally sighed with relief. And then I could see the look of confusion on the face of the second baseman, and I already knew I was doing the wrong thing. But for some reason I couldn't stop. I tossed the ball underhand to second.

"*What are you doing?*" Ron yelled. No, make that "screamed," and in front my girlfriend and the rest of the team. As for me, I didn't know what to say. It would have been a bonehead play in any league, from t-ball to the majors, and I knew it. Still, I felt the need to defend myself.

"You, you said to throw it to second..." I stammered weakly.

"That was on the *last* play!" Ron screamed unnecessarily. I already knew that.

Well, we did finally manage to get three outs, and while I don't remember who actually won that game, I think it's a pretty safe bet that it wasn't us. Oh, and that was the end of my career at shortstop.

So anyone would agree that in the grand scheme of things a throwing error in a game of softball doesn't rate very high on the list of life's little horrors. And yet every time I think of this incident I cringe inside, and wish there was some way I could go back in time and do things differently.

Here's the odd part, though. Thinking about that unrealistic opportunity to relive this experience, I become a little confused. I'm not really sure which part of it I would change. Would I not throw that ball to second base, would I not give that feeble excuse right after I had or would I just go ahead and knock Ron on his big fat ass?

Leonard Stegmann

The Snow Shovel

For once the weather report hadn't let us down. The prediction said the snow would continue to fall throughout the day, and that's exactly what it had done. And now my childhood chum Lenny and I, still exuberant from enjoying the rare and glorious snow day that had closed our school, had come up with a way to make a little cash besides.

And so we walked the mile up Broadway, struggling through the freshly fallen foot of snow, and eventually huffed and puffed our way to the train station. It was late afternoon, and we, in our wisdom, knew that the trains from the city would soon be coming through, spitting out their cargo of harried businessmen. These men had left for work early that morning, when they were fresh and full of energy, and their cars had not yet been buried in snow. And Lenny and I, well, we had brought our snow shovels.

"Dig out your car for a dollar?" we asked each commuter as we followed him to his car. It seemed like a foolproof plan. After all, what were their options? To our way of thinking these exhausted businessmen had the choice of either availing themselves of our rather inexpensive service or spending a cold uncomfortable night in the back seat of their stuck cars. Really, what else could they possibly do?

As it turned out we didn't quite have the dominant market position we thought we did. Nearly everyone told us, "No, thank you." The responses were both polite and nearly unanimous. The snow, as it turned out, hadn't created quite the impenetrable barriers that we had thought, and hoped, it would. Most of the drivers, by gunning the motor and spinning the wheels, were able to eventually back out of their parking space. It was a bit reckless, but highly effective. One or two of the more clever types (clearly they were management material) had actually had the forethought to stash a snow shovel in their trunk.

Soon the parking lot was nearly empty, the gray sky began to darken and an icy wind started to blow. Lenny and I had to admit that our master plan had not quite yielded the riches we had hoped for. In fact, in the three hours we were there we had shoveled out only one car, for which we had earned fifty cents apiece. Still, we weren't quite ready to give it up, and so when we saw a man walking towards his snow-bound car we ran towards him.

"Dig out your car for a dollar?" we asked.

"Can I borrow your shovel?" he replied.

"We can do it for you, for a dollar," we repeated.

"CAN I BORROW YOUR SHOVEL?" *he* repeated, this time louder, making it sound more like a command than a request.

We were raised to be polite boys and to respect our elders, and he was, after all, an adult. And a big, persuasive one at that. And so we did what was clearly expected of us: We handed over one of our shovels. The man went right to work, and inside of a minute he had energetically cleared enough snow to allow him to easily back out his car. He handed the shovel back to us, and I'd like to think he said "thank you." And then he was gone.

Lenny and I went to the corner candy store to get out of the cold, sat at the counter and ordered hot chocolate. True, the fifteen cents we each spent on the chocolate was nearly a third of our day's wages, but that was okay. The steaming beverage was warming and delicious, made even more so because we had bought it with money that we ourselves had earned. All too soon the last now-tepid drops were swallowed and it was time to pick up our shovels, return to the snowy, dark night and begin the long trek to our homes.

Lenny and I still talk about this day every now and again. Sure, some of the details have faded into the mists of half a century, but there is one incident we both recall quite clearly. It is, of course, that guy who, rather than pay a couple of enterprising kids to dig out his car, had instead bullied them into handing him their shovel. We laugh about it now, and have for years. We invariably end the story with one, and sometimes both, of us remembering that man with the same three words.

"What a prick," we always say.

Leonard Stegmann

Undefeated

"And of course I never play if there are only children sitting there. I mean, I'm not a monster. But if I see a string of adults lined up, or even if it's just *mostly* adults, I'll plop myself right down and grab that pistol. And I'll win, too. Every time."

This was me, pontificating to my visiting brother as we strolled along the midway at the county fair. We were approaching that carnival game where you shoot water into a clown's mouth, causing a balloon to expand over its head. The first person to get his balloon to break wins a prize. First shelf only, please.

The truth was that, while perhaps I didn't win at the game every single time, I won more often than not. My secret was simple. I employed a Zen-like focus, aiming the pistol at the target even before the water stream was turned on, and then held the stream steady until the game was over. I didn't let that stream waver an inch, and I didn't at any time look away to see who might be winning or gaining on me, not even for a second.

And so, without saying a word, my brother sat on one of the colorful stools, paid the man and picked up a pistol. I did the same thing, about two stools down. (I don't like to be crowded when I'm shootin'.) And a very short time later the balloon over my brother's clown burst. First. He chose some kind of toy stuffed rodent, from the first shelf of course, and handed it to my wife. All without saying a word.

I should have immediately challenged him again. I know that now. But I didn't, and so for the rest of the day at the fair, and for the rest of his vacation, it just hung in the air like smog: my little brother had beaten me at the water balloon game; *my* water balloon game.

 And yet I always knew that, through some bizarre set of circumstances I couldn't even begin to imagine, my brother and I would someday find ourselves together again on a fair's midway, competing in that water balloon game. And this time I would win. And I'd continue to win every time we ever happened to play the game, forever.

That highly anticipated rematch never took place, however. It seemed terribly unfair, almost like cheating, when a few months later my brother took his own life. I would never get my chance to even the score, as my brother had suddenly and dramatically chosen to retire from the water balloon game. Undefeated.

Leonard Stegmann

They Call Me Arroz Con Pollo

"This is my first meal in South America," said the old man on my TV screen. I was watching a movie from the 1950's. The old man's next line was, "I think I'll have the arroz con pollo. I've always wanted to try that." And with the unexpected mention of arroz con pollo I was immediately transported back to my eighth grade Spanish class, and made to laugh out loud as well.

We were having a quiz. A simple one. Actually it was the format of the quiz that was simple, not its content. Not for me, anyway. Our teacher, Mr. Thornton, excuse me, I mean *Senor*

Thorton, would read aloud a short story in Spanish, and would then ask us ten questions about the story, also in Spanish.

I didn't have particularly high hopes *before* the quiz started, and once the story had ended I realized in a combination of chagrin and outright horror that I had understood almost nothing at all. I was pretty sure we had just heard a narrative about a family having dinner, but who they were or what they talked about I hadn't a clue. All I knew for sure was that I had heard the phrase "arroz con pollo," and cleverly deduced that this was what the family was eating.

And so the questions began, and I became even more lost. When the quiz was done I was dismayed to see that my ten "answers" were little more than a list of guesses and blank spaces. The most glaring absurdity, however, was that I had written "arroz con pollo" as an answer…four times.

I knew, of course, that one of the questions Senor Thornton had asked in Spanish was, "What did the family have for dinner?" The problem was, I didn't have a clue which question it had been. I guess I figured I had four chances to at least get this one question correct.

Mr. Thornton returned our graded quizzes the next day. I honestly don't remember if I had actually hit the right question on any of my "arroz con pollo" answers, but I do know that Mr. Thornton got quite a good laugh out my attempt.

And so that day a nickname was born. For the rest of the year Mr. Thornton would know me as "arroz con pollo," and not just in class but any time we might happen to pass in the halls as well. In fact, I have no doubt that he told my story to many, if not all, of his future classes, right up until the day he retired. Which was fine. Mr. Thornton was a good teacher and a sweet man.

Forty-six years later I sat down and looked at the menu in an open-air café in Costa Rica. There were a lot of delicious sounding items listed, but my decision was made the second I saw it. The arroz con pollo was quite good; so good, in fact, that I would order it again a few days later. Still, I couldn't help but smile, and think back to Mr. Thornton's long-ago Spanish class, as I tasted my first bite of the dish I had first heard of almost half a century earlier. In some strange and amusing way, I knew I had come full circle.

That Won't Do You Any Good

Putting the Lights on the Christmas Tree

When I was growing up it was always Dad's job to put the lights on the Christmas tree, and he did it efficiently and unerringly year after year. He'd then retire downstairs to watch football on TV while his three sons decorated the tree with a colorful assortment of ornaments, garland and much too much tinsel. Looking back, it was a simple system and it worked just fine.

It has been my job to string the lights for many years now, and while it's not a chore I relish I still manage to accomplish the task with a minimum of angst and offensive language. Unlike Dad, however, I don't disappear when I'm done, but hang around to assist my wife with the final decorating. Incidentally, both garland and tinsel have gone the way of the dodo bird over the last decade or so, so it's somewhat simpler task than it was fifty years ago. Except for those damn lights.

There's a new device I saw on television that allows you to store your Christmas lights in a way that they don't get all tangled. We don't have that device. And this year, for whatever reason, the lights took *forever* (probably about three and a half minutes) to get straightened out. Once that was done I started at the top of the tree and wound the first string of lights around and around until it ran out about halfway down the tree, as it should. Perfect.

Then I did something I don't usually do—I plugged in the lights and they looked lovely, just as you'd expect. And then, feeling a little guilty, I unplugged them. You see, the idea is to put on both strings of lights, and hopefully all the decorations, before you turn on the lights. You want to get that full effect all at once. At least *I* do. You, of course, may have your own way of doing things. And if so, you're wrong.

And so I proceeded to wind the second set of lights around the lower portion of the tree and then I plugged in both sets. Nothing. I tried both the upper and the lower wall sockets and not a single spot of light appeared anywhere on the tree. This was curious, as I had already tested the first string, which you'd know if you've been paying attention at all. So even if there was something defective in the second string of lights, it should have no effect on the first.

I'm sure I uttered something foul, because Spike was soon in the room, asking me what was wrong. I calmly (as far as you know) explained that neither set of lights was working, emphasizing how long it had taken me to string them just right. I'm not certain, but another coarse word might have slipped out at some point.

"I bought some new lights that are still in the package," Spike offered.

I don't clearly remember what my response was, but I hope I didn't simply ignore her. I'd like to think I'm better than that. (I'm not, but I'd like to think it.) I *do* know I was thinking that I wasn't about to put myself through the agony of taking down not one, but *two* strings of perfectly placed lights, and then putting up two new ones. Instead I would follow the flow of the electricity and thus pinpoint the location of this problem. Didn't we learn something like that working with those giant nine-volt batteries in third grade?

First I tested the extension cord. The way you do this, for those of you at home who are less electronically adept, is to take the cord to another outlet. I chose the one in the bathroom. I plugged it in and then plugged the hairdryer into that. And a second later I was, quite accidentally, shooting a blast of hot air right into my face, and blowing a contact lens right into the sink. It was not, as you might imagine, a pleasant sensation.

Next I took the hairdryer to the outlet by the Christmas tree and plugged it in there. Again the hairdryer instantly came to life. This time, however, I had the foresight to not only be wearing my glasses, but to turn the damn thing away from my face. So sorry to disappoint you.

And so now I knew that, as both the extension cord and the outlets (not to mention the hairdryer) were working fine, the problem was clearly in the lights themselves. I related to Spike how I had, by careful use of the scientific method, cleverly deduced exactly where, if not what, the problem was. She was a lot less impressed than you might expect.

"I left those new lights over there on the chair," she said.

I, course, having two sets of lights already on the tree, said nothing. Nothing she could hear, anyway. And then I began to methodically inspect one string of lights and found a bulb was missing. Of course! These things don't work at all if there's a missing bulb. Right? I think I remember that from about twenty years ago.

And so I found an extra bulb, put it in the empty socket and plugged in. Nothing. I guess strings of Christmas lights haven't really worked that way since, well, since Dad was in charge. I was pretty much at a loss at this point, and so began to unwrap the first string of lights from the upper part of the tree. You know, the lights that had worked twenty minutes ago but didn't now. When I got them down I brought them over to the outlet and plugged them in.

"That's impossible!" I yelled loud enough to send the cat to a distant, more peaceful, part of the house. I mean, how could they not light up on the tree when plugged into a clearly-working extension cord, but yet light up now? It didn't make any sense. This is *not* what they taught us in third grade.

"Those new boxes of lights I bought are still in their wrappers," said Spike.

You know, it's late right now and I don't really have time to go online and look this up. But if I did, I bet I'd discover that I wouldn't be the first person ever to strangle his or her mate with a string of Christmas lights. Why not do the research yourself? You'll see that I'm right.

And so in the end I took the second string of lights off the tree, plugged it in to find out it still didn't work and then wound both sets of lights tightly together and threw them into the trash. I then opened the two sets of new lights, which I was lucky to have, and repeated the irritating process of wrapping lights around the Christmas tree. I then closed the drapes to darken the room, plugged in the lights and took a step or two back to admire my handiwork. It looked nice. I think Dad would have been proud.

Leonard Stegmann

T.P.

❧❧❧❧❧

Full disclosure: Up until a few months ago I had no idea where the toilet paper was kept in this house. I only knew that there was always a roll on the roller, and when that ran out I could reach into the drawer under the sink—without getting up!—and there, without fail, would be a new roll waiting for me.

Now, I could claim that I had no idea where this toilet paper comes from, but really, since there are only two of us living here, and since I stopped believing in toilet paper elves when I hit my forties, that claim would be absurd.

On top of that, I haven't actually bought a roll of toilet paper in over a decade. And while it might at first seem unfair that it should fall to Spike to buy 100% of the toilet paper we use, I ask you to withhold your judgment. You see, I estimate that Spike also *uses* over 90% of it.

I replaced a roll just yesterday. Today I found that it was almost completely used up. And since, again, there are only two people in the house, and it wasn't me who used up an entire roll in less than twenty-four hours, it doesn't take a Columbo to identify the culprit. And she's not even here during the day!

How does somebody go through this much toilet paper? Does she wrap it around and around her hand as if she beginning some delicate and ancient mummification process, or taping up for her big Tyson fight? Now, have I seen her do this? Well, no, but I've seen her at work with the paper towels in the kitchen, and it doesn't take much to extrapolate from there.

And I'll take it a step further. I suspect the excessive use of toilet paper is not something limited to my own house, but is the general practice of women everywhere. Not that there's not some justification for it. A woman, because of the curious way she is built, finds it necessary to use toilet paper every time she uses the bathroom. Men just use it for, how can I put this delicately without sounding like a grade-schooler? I can't. Men just use it when we go Number Two. Women also use it for Number One. They dab.

I remember a woman years ago who was surprised that men, generally speaking, don't dab. Is that because we are, by nature, the most disgusting of creatures? We are, of course, but that's not the reason. Without getting too graphic, it only takes us a shake or two. It's not a question of right or wrong, Ladies, it's a question of your inferior plumbing fixtures. And if you balked at the word "inferior," well, let's just save that discussion for another time. Perhaps the next time you're in a line of twenty women waiting to use the restroom?

So Spike, I guess, thought she had it all figured out. She assumed that if she buys all the toilet paper then she could use as much as she wants, whenever she wants, without having to hear any complaints about it. Why would she ever think that? She must have had some kind of mental lapse and forgotten who she's living with.

That Won't Do You Any Good

Tapa the Food Chain

I never stood a chance. And yet somehow I was still surprised when the flight attendant told me that all they had left was the Savory box. I told her nah, I'd rather buy one of your desiccated chicken sandwiches, which I did.

They sell three kinds of snack boxes on United Airlines flights: Savory, Classic and Tapas. I was sitting in Row 28 and had been waiting over an hour for the food card to rumble its way back to me and my fellow riff-raff at the back of the plane. And when it did, well you already read what happened.

I had wanted the Tapas snack box, badly, and it had never crossed my mind that they could run out of them. I have yet to learn, apparently, that an airplane is not like a restaurant. They carry just a very limited selection of food, and if you happen to be seated in one of the knee-and-soul-crushing rows towards the rear of the plane, well, you take what you get.

You might be asking yourself if the three snack boxes are really that much different. No, certainly no more different than, say, Katy Perry and Gaylord Perry. The Savory snack box, to my way of thinking, is the worst of the fleet. For $7.49, here's what you get: Tortilla Chips, Salsa, Vanilla Raspberry Fig Bar, Almonds, Nutella , Graham Crackers and Dried Fruit. And don't get me wrong. If I had just crawled upon one of these after fifteen days in the desert, why sure, I'd eat it. At least, after all the lizards and scorpions were gone.

Now the Classic is actually the same price as the Savory, but so much better, at least to my way of thinking. With this snack box you get Applesauce, Pepperidge Farm Goldfish, Crackers, Pepperoni, Cheddar Cheese Spread, Candy and Oreo Cookies. Okay, goldfish, pepperoni and even candy. Now we're getting somewhere!

But it's the Tapas snack box that I always crave. Sure, it's about a buck more but you know what? A Mercedes costs more than a Ford, and there's a damn good reason why. Here's what you'll enjoy if you're fortunate enough to find yourself crammed into your airplane seat with a Tapas snack box: Marinated Olives, Roasted Red Pepper Bruschetta Spread, Wild Garden Hummus, Parmesan Cheese Spread, Pita Chips, Cream Crackers, Olive Oil and Sea Salt Crackers, Almonds and Chocolate Covered Fruit.

Are you kidding me? I mean, I need only pop open one of these babies and I'm once again on the island of Santorini, eating the most incredible lunch as I happily gaze down upon the impossibly blue waters of the Aegean Sea.

"Do you want to take some meatball sandwiches with you for the plane?" Dad had asked.

"No thanks." I answered. You must be kidding. I had been thinking about that Tapas snack box since I'd woken up that morning. I remembered everything about it, except, of course, the fact that I had gotten shut out on the flight coming here.

A few hours later I was on the return flight, this time in Row 29, even further back than the flight I had taken a week earlier. And again the elbow-banging food cart was rolled past me and to the special people up front; the ones with both the extra leg room *and* the first crack at the snack boxes.

I returned to my book, almost forgetting about my Tapas snack box, which I knew was over an hour away. *If* I was lucky. Time passed and eventually the food cart was only about five rows ahead. I squinted through my ten dollar online-bought glasses to assess the situation. Either my cheap spectacles were playing tricks on me or there were two, no *three*, Tapas boxes still on the cart! Oh happy day!

Still, I've never been one to count pre-hatched poultry, and so I watched with Zen-like focus as the flight attendant asked each passenger if they'd like to buy a meal. To my surprise, and barely suppressed glee, most of the people said no. Ha! They probably all had carry-on bags stuffed with dripping meatball sandwiches. Too bad, losers!

With but two rows to go I found myself answering, although under my breath, for each person who was asked if they wanted any food. No, you don't. No, thanks. You don't need any, Tubby. And then a thought hit me. What if there was only *one* Tapas left by the time they got to my row?

You see, I wasn't flying alone. My wife Spike was sitting to my left and she, too, had mentioned that she wanted a Tapas snack box. So what would happen if there was only one left? Would I do the gentlemanly thing and let Spike have it? Yeah right, and then I'd sprout wings and fly the rest of the way to San Francisco under my own power. Would we flip a coin? Admittedly I'd feel pretty bad if I had to eat my Tapas with Spike sitting there watching me, but I'd feel a lot worse if it was *me* who had to watch *her*.

And then it happened. The flight attendant, who had just become the most beautiful woman in the world, was asking me if I wanted to buy a meal. I could see the three boxes of Tapas sitting atop her cart, and I did my best to control my excitement, and to answer her in a clear and distinct manner, as if I was speaking to a cop who had just asked me if I'd been drinking.

"I'd like the Tapas box, please," I said. And then she handed it to me.

When you look at the list of treats in the Tapas box it's tempting to think that they have included too many chips and crackers. That kind of reasoning is an amateur, and possibly dangerous, mistake. For the next half hour I created the most delicious combinations, making my gastronomical orgy even more delectable than I had anticipated. I put hummus on a pita chip, and topped it with an olive. I spread a bit of parmesan cheese on a sea salt cracker and popped an olive on *that*. I put both the bruschetta spread *and* hummus on a cream cracker. Did I mention the chocolate covered fruit?

At one point I took a short break from the feast, leaned back in the seat and sighed happily. I thought of my friend Joe, who always seemed to have a fine appreciation of life's pleasures, even the little ones. Joe wasn't with me on this flight, of course, but if he had been I know what he'd say. It was something he said often, especially at blissful occasions such as this one. Joe would have said, "Man, this is living."

Leonard Stegmann

The China Syndrome

"Okay then, how about this? We'll go to Target and buy a bunch of new dishes and I'll put an "S" on each one with a Magic Marker?" This was me, desperately, and wittily I thought, attempting to get out of doing something I didn't want to do. I knew I didn't stand a chance.

"Your mother told me about five times that I was going to get those dishes. She wanted me to have them…" said Spike, repeating again what I already knew and had long ago accepted.

You see, I was in Florida emptying out my parents' home before selling it. Spike was on the other side of the country. When the house was sold I would be driving back to California, and it was beginning to look like those five giant boxes of china would be coming with me.

We're really not china people. My mother had several sets, one of which would come out whenever part of the family, which could be anywhere from four to over twenty people, came by to visit. Spike and I, on the other hand, are not quite as sociable. By way of illustration, imagine that we've lived next door to a

That Won't Do You Any Good

very nice couple for thirteen years now. We've never been inside their house, and we're still not quite sure about the wife's first name. (And we have no idea about their last.)

Needless to say, we don't need plates for a seating of ten people. And we sure as hell don't need ten coffee cups, and their saucers to boot. Spike doesn't drink coffee and I have a very serviceable mug, complete with a picture of Crow T. Robot.

I looked at the pile of stuff on the living room floor. This is what I would be driving back to California. I had whittled it down pretty good, I thought, but that damn boxes of china took up so much room. And so I grabbed one of the boxes and brought it to the shipping store on the corner. I had been sending various mementos and other assorted bric-a-brac to even more assorted relatives for the past few weeks. The owner of the place thought I was his new best friend. Why not simply mail one of the boxes of china to Spike?

My new best friend told me that packing and shipping the box would cost about seventy dollars. Would I like insurance? No, I wouldn't. It's not like it a box of, oh, I don't know, Beatles albums. And off went the first set of dishes. I felt lighter already.

And so over the next two weeks, each time I felt a lull in activities, I brought another box of china to the shipping store. It wasn't long before Spike reported that they had started to arrive.

"You're just going to leave them in the garage until we die, you know," I said cheerfully.

"I know," she agreed.

But she didn't. Today, having returned to California a month ago, we decided to do something really outrageous. After spending bemoaning the fact that we had no progeny to dump any of our crap on (the cat was only interested in snacks) we decided hey, why don't we use the china ourselves. And not just for special occasions, but all the time? And so we spent today unpacking the dishes, bowls and yes, even the coffee cups and saucers and replaced all of our old, chipped plates, bowls and mugs. (No, not the Crow T. Robot one. Are you insane?)

We didn't stop there either. I had also brought back a set of silverware. This was the real stuff—not silver-plated or silver-colored. And so we cleaned out our collection of mismatched and bent stainless of forks, knives and spoons and filled the plastic organizer with the good stuff.

We had spaghetti and fish sticks for dinner tonight. This was topped off with a couple of scoops of chocolate-chip ice cream. Nothing fancy, mind you, but I'll be damned if it all didn't taste better when eaten with forks and spoons made of pure silver. Oh, and plates of real china that had an "S" on them.

Leonard Stegmann

The All-Star Game Is Tonight

I was clicking around the dial last night (As if TV's still have dials. Or click.) and noticed that the Home Run Derby was on. That's right, I said to myself, the All-Star Game is tomorrow. You know, I didn't even bother to watch the Home Run Derby, not even for a second.

There was a time when the All-Star Game mattered quite a bit to me, and to my childhood chum Lenny. Lenny was a Yankees fan, and so rooted for the American League team. I was stuck haplessly cheering for the Mets, and so the National League was my team. Not that I had much of a chance of actually seeing a Met in an All-Star Game during those years. (That all changed in 1969, of course. At least temporarily.)

Here in the Bay Area we have two teams, and I root for both of them. Namby-pamby stuff like that would never have flown back then in New York. No, you either rooted for the Yankees *or* you rooted for the Mets. Anyone who ever dared to admit that he "kinda liked them both" (and I never met a single person who did) was sure to be heaped from each side with fetid piles of scorn and disgust.

That Won't Do You Any Good

I don't remember where Lenny and I were going that night, but I know our dads had taken us and our brothers *somewhere*. I do remember that it was the night of the All-Star Game. And so we waited outside of whatever event we were attending, Lenny and I desperately trying to hear the All-Star Game through the tinny, quarter-sized speaker of a cheap transistor radio.

The Mets might actually have had somebody in an All-Star Game, or they might not. The Yankees, of course, most certainly would. And it was always a big thrill when the representative of *your* team came up to bat, or was called in to pitch. And if he happened to get a clutch hit, or maybe chalk up a crucial strikeout, well, you'd be bursting with a youthful, and totally unearned, pride for the rest of the week.

Another nice thing about the All-Star Game, especially for a Mets fan of that time, was that all of the players that you feared all season long were, at least for this one night, on your team. Once a year Bob Gibson might be pitching and you could root for him. Willie Mays might hit a homerun and you'd be free to cheer.

And this temporary and short-lived sense of relief was never more pronounced than when San Francisco Giant Willie McCovey came to bat. Year in and year out, McCovey would pound the Mets into the well-groomed dust of Shea Stadium. I once got to a game early enough to sneak down to field level and watch batting practice. I stood transfixed, only a few feet from McCovey, as he sent ball after ball deep into the right field stands. I was so close, and he generated so much raw power, that I didn't know whether to cry or wet my pants. And what he'd be doing to my beloved Mets in about half an hour would probably cause me to do both.

The All-Star Game is being played right now as I write this. Maybe when I'm done here I'll give it a look. Or maybe I won't. I'll probably end up watching some *30 Rock* reruns instead. The truth is I don't care very much about the All-Star Game, and haven't for decades. And a part of me thinks that's too bad, because I still remember those times when Lenny and I practically lived and died based on who won the All-Star Game. We cared *so* very much.

That Bitch!

It was only Public Access but it was still looked like fun. I had seen a notice on TV announcing that classes were beginning at the local television station. "Learn TV Production!" it had proclaimed. Well, I thought to myself, that sounds like it might be interesting. And so I called the number and signed right up.

It was a six-week course, made up of a string of Saturday classes that lasted two hours. Oh, who am I kidding? I don't know how long the classes lasted. Maybe it was one hour and maybe it was three. It was a long time ago.

After completing the first two weeks the instructor informed us that we were now qualified to operate the cameras for the station's productions. Other skills would be taught, and hopefully acquired, in the weeks to come. Normally, we were told, we'd have a small badge to wear in the studio, but they hadn't yet come back from the printer.

"Just tell whoever is running the show that I said it's okay for you guys to work the cameras," said the instructor.

I thought I'd give it a shot, and so volunteered to work on the crew for a program later that week. When I showed up I was assigned one of the three cameras, and immediately began to practice what I'd been taught. It was pretty simple really: zoom in, zoom out, pan left, pan right. Nothing to it. We were about ten minutes to air time, and I was raring to go, when I was approached by this girl. She was the station employee who would be in charge that night.

"Do you have your badge?" she asked me.

And so I explained that the badges hadn't come in yet, but the instructor had said it was okay for our class to operate the cameras.

"Well, you can't work on the crew if you don't have a badge," she said. "That's the rule," she added, unnecessarily I thought.

Now I was getting pissed off. I had come all the way from my home to work as a volunteer for their silly TV show, and now this chick was going to tell me I couldn't do it? Well, I was about ten years older than she was, and so had a lot more experience dealing with this kind of bullshit. I'd be setting her straight, and pretty darn quick, too.

Except I didn't. The bitch actually pulled me off camera and I spent the evening watching the show from inside of the control room. It just goes to show you, you give some people a little bit of power, even a young girl in her twenties, and it goes right to their heads.

I soon calmed down, of course, and spent most of the time talking to the girl who had pulled me off the camera. I got to see how the show was produced from inside the control room, and it turned out to be not such a bad evening after all.

I went on to finish the television production course, but rarely worked on a crew. I ended up in front of the camera for over twenty years, which was where I had really wanted to be in the first place. I'm sorry that I can't tell you exactly where that girl who pulled me off the camera is today. I *can*, however, tell you where she'll be tonight. We're going out to dinner for our fifteenth wedding anniversary.

Leonard Stegmann

That White Piece of Paper

While I don't remember exactly what the threatened consequences were for losing that white piece of paper, I do recall that they had seemed quite dire. If I'm not mistaken they included excessive fines, a not-inconsequential prison term and the possible application of an assortment of Bush Era-style tortures.

Okay, so maybe it wasn't as bad as all that, but I know that when I received that white slip of paper from Peruvian immigration I was told I had better not lose it. Or else. And so now, along with the usual subtle, but constant, anxiety of worrying about losing my passport, I now also had the added pressure of making sure that the piece of paper was still there every time I checked.

Which was often. And now, unlike on other visits to foreign lands, I could not just reach into my pocket or pack and simply *feel* that the passport was there. No, that was now only half of the search. I would have to actually take out the passport, open it up, and check to make sure that paper was where I had put it.

Did I ever open my passport, not see it immediately and feel that special chill that shoots down the spine when you think, "Oh my god! I've lost it!" Yes, and on more than one occasion. And to remind me that losing the paper was always a very real possibility, I actually looked down at my feet one time and saw the paper *lying there on the floor!* I had dropped it while being subjected to the stress and humiliation of an airport security screening.

And yet, even though I carried around this very important piece of paper for over a week, I never actually took a good look at it. I do know that it was very official looking, bore one or two quite authoritative stamps, as well as a signature written by somebody who clearly knew what he was doing. I wasn't even sure what the paper was for, but I think basically it was the government of Peru giving me permission -- for a limited amount of time, mind you -- to stumble around their country and look at stuff. As long as I hung onto this highly important piece of paper, that is.

It was at the third airport security checkpoint, as I began the process of leaving Peru, that somebody at long last asked for that white piece of paper. It's an exaggeration, of course, to say that the feeling of relieving myself of that piece of paper was similar to dropping a fifty-pound pack after a grueling hike, but less of an exaggeration than you might think.

And, to be honest, along with that sense of relief I must admit I felt a bit of pride. I had done it! I had carried around that white piece of paper for my entire trip, kept it safe and then had triumphantly delivered it to the serious-looking uniformed official upon request. And to think there were people in my life who told me that I would never, ever, succeed at anything.

That Won't Do You Any Good

Peter Pan

They're at it again. A new version of the musical *Peter Pan* is going to be on TV this week, and once again the part of the boy who wouldn't grow up is played by a woman, as it has been for over 100 years. Oh yes, the first stage production based on J.M. Barrie's popular and, dare we say, somewhat annoying, character took place in the closing days of 1904.

In that play Peter Pan was portrayed by an actress named Maude Adams. I myself, no matter what you may suspect, do not go back quite that far, but my aged old brain does contain some fuzzy memories of watching Mary Martin on TV in the musical version of *Peter Pan* several times as a kid. I wasn't that big a fan.

First of all, I never found the story particularly compelling. I didn't care much about the Lost Boys, Captain Hook or even Peter himself. And then there was something about a crocodile with a ticking clock in its stomach that I didn't quite get back then, and am not sure that I do now.

But mostly it was that woman swooping around above the stage. I never for a second bought the idea that I was watching a young boy flying, and always knew that this was a grown-up woman playing the part of Peter Pan. I just didn't know why. And it was because of this that I was completely taken out of the story.

I mean, I might not have been a child genius, but I was pretty confident in my ability to tell the difference between a young boy and a forty-six year old woman. So why did I watch *Peter Pan* several times over the years? There were two reasons: That's what the family was watching on our sole TV set, and we only had about five clear channels anyway.

Other women have gone on to play Peter Pan on the stage, including Sandy Duncan, Cathy Rigby and now Allison Williams later this week. It's been said that Peter is always played by a woman because it has become a theatrical tradition. Well, the nice thing about traditions is that they can be broken. And the time to break this one is now.

I am often amazed by the acting abilities of, well, all actors really, but especially the very young. Many of them were nominated for an Academy Award before they'd even entered their teens. So surely, surely there must be at least one young male actor out there under the age of, say, sixteen, who is capable of handling the role of Peter Pan? Of course there is.

So let's get this done. And once we set up this tradition it just might bring a new generation of fans to this already admittedly beloved musical. And best of all, we will have done a good deed for future generations, knowing that now when a young boy goes to bed after watching the play he doesn't have to lie awake all night, confused as to why he found himself more attracted to Peter Pan than to, you know, Wendy. Or even Tinkerbell.

Leonard Stegmann

Opposite Day

ఞఞఞఞఞ

It's not because some nutty old white man in the sky is pulling your strings like a marionette, nor is it "The Universe" doing everything in its power to make all of your silly hopes and wishes come true. No, it's a pretty random walk out there, Folks. And that's why it can be so much fun when something lines up in a pattern, even if only for a minute or two.

There are 7 billion of us dupes stumbling around this forlorn rock of ours, and every day each of us performs hundreds of actions and has thousands of thoughts. (Well, most of us, anyway.) So, as you can see, there's going to be an occasional alignment that seems amazing or other-worldly. In fact it's just a "coincidence," and they can sometimes be a quite entertaining. Here's mine for the week:

Sunday started out agreeable enough, with the Oakland A's completing a sweep of the nearly collapsed Texas Rangers. Nothing, it now seems, will stop the A's from taking first place in their division. I was quite content with the outcome, and now was ready for some football.

In my head I had already written my snide Facebook comment, destined for a couple of my Raider fan friends. After the Raiders inevitable loss and the Niners win I would post: "I guess the only question now is if the Raiders will win more games this season than the Niners will win in their first month." Pretty slick, huh?

But then something funny happened, and I don't mean humorous funny. The Raiders *won* their game. Sure, they were playing one of the more hapless teams in the NFL, but I'm too big a person to actually mention that in print. And by now I suppose you've figured out that the Niners went on to lose their game later that evening. Well, perhaps lose is an understatement, in that my team "lost" in Seattle in much the same way Custer "lost" at the Little Big Horn.

Clearly my snippy comment was of no use now, but I had to post something, right? And so I got on Facebook and, like the sore-loser that I am, I wrote: "The Raiders win and the Niners lose? It must be Opposite Day!"

I was pretty happy with that line, I must say. And then I thought about it and began to wonder: Exactly what *is* Opposite Day? I'd heard the expression somewhere, of course, perhaps on TV show or two. And so I looked it up and here's what I discovered.

It seems that Opposite Day is an unofficial holiday, but that's not the amazing part. On Opposite Day people will say the exact opposite of what they mean. I mean, more than usual. Opposite Day has indeed been referenced in various places in the media, including in an episode of *Spongebob Squarepants*, although I can't begin to imagine how I could have possibly seen it there. Ahem. But that's still not the amazing part.

It turns out that there is an official day of the year that is associated with Opposite Day, and that day is Septemeber 15th. Yes, the very same September 15th, last Sunday, on which the Raiders won and the Niners lost, and I made my oh-so-witty comment. So, you have to agree that the fact that it really *was* Opposite day was quite a coincidence!

What, you don't agree? You don't even see what the big deal is? Hey listen, Chump, do me a favor and check back here next September 15th. I want to tell you what an unspeakable joy it is to knock out this literary compost for you every damn day of my life.

That Won't Do You Any Good

Roger and Me

Father Tom didn't live on our block, but his sister did. And so he would periodically come by to visit. And on several of these occasions he would be accompanied by a young, freckle-faced boy of about my age, which was eleven, named Roger.

Being eleven, I never did get a clear picture of the situation until many years later. In truth, I still have some gaps in my understanding of what went on, but I'd like to think at this point I have, at least, the gist of it.

Roger, I assume, was some troubled kid from "the city." What his "trouble" might have been nobody ever told me, and I never asked, but it doesn't take a particularly creative imagination to conceive of the potentially horrible possibilities. Hell, it might only have been something as seemingly innocuous as his parents getting a divorce, which was an event both rarer and more traumatic fifty years ago than it is today.

Whatever the reason, it was obvious that Father Tom had taken Roger under his wing to try to help the kid out. Which is fine, and even admirable. What wasn't so fine, however, was Father Tom using my chum Lenny and me to aid him in his quest to heal Roger. You see, unlike Father Tom, we hadn't signed on to become professional do-gooders. And, also unlike Father Tom, we weren't getting paid.

The whole process, as I recall, was rather slyly orchestrated. It was first presented to us as some sort of great treat, or reward, although what Lenny and I were being rewarded for I couldn't begin to imagine. Father Tom had arrived and he was going to take Lenny and I (and Roger, of course) over to the schoolyard to play baseball!

Now, Lenny and I played baseball, in one form or another, nearly every day of our lives, weather permitting. And we played right in front of our houses. So driving over to the schoolyard, with Father Tom and his goofy little protégé, barely registered a beep on our excitement meters.

But we went anyway. And in truth, we hadn't been told by anyone that we *had* to go, but I also don't recall realistically having a say in the matter. You see, Father Tom was, of course, a priest, and what eleven year old Catholic boy is going to say "no" to one of those? Remember, this was a time when they were frying people in Hell for all eternity for such crimes as eating a hamburger on Friday. No, if Father Tom wanted us to go to the schoolyard and play baseball with wacky

That Won't Do You Any Good

Roger, well, by God, that's exactly what we were going to do.

Was it fun? Not particularly. And while I also don't remember throwing the ball around as being something dreadful, it seems to me it felt like more of an obligation than anything else. After all, what kind of baseball game could you have with three kids and a decrepit (well into his 30's) old priest?

What I remember most about Roger, however, was not those ill-attempted and dreary baseball games, but rather the rides to and from the schoolyard. Father Tom, forever and desperately trying to generate good cheer, would try to get us all singing. He was very pleased when Roger would sing what Father Tom considered a "nice" song. As for me, I don't recall singing very much at all. I just wanted to get back home.

The song for which Roger received the most approval from Father Tom was one from the 1930's called "Goody Goody." And it was during these performances, by Roger from the front seat of the car, that I started to notice that he was more than just some nutty inner-city kid; he could also be kind of funny.

Roger would start off by singing "Goody Goody," and just when Father Tom, behind the steering wheel, had been lulled into a toe-tapping near-stupor, Roger would suddenly raise his voice and switch tunes, practically shouting, "I want to hold your ha-a-a-a-n-n-d!" as he played an imaginary guitar.

"Roger!" Father Tom would yell, and then spend the next ten minutes or so trying to convince the irrepressible redhead to "sing something nice." Which, as you can imagine, got *me* a little agitated. Not that I would ever say anything to contradict a priest, but who was he, really, to decide that a bit of treacle like "Goody Goody" was superior in any way to a Beatles song? It was 1964, dammit, and most of us kids thought that "I Want to Hold Your Hand" was something "nice." *Really* nice.

I don't think that Father Tom dragged us over to that schoolyard to play ball, and to socialize Roger, more than three times, or so. I do know that, while I never refused to go, I slowly became aware that I was being used, and resented it a little more each time. And yet, from where I sit today, I realize Father Tom was nothing but well-intentioned, and really did me no harm at all. And as for Roger, well, he was no doubt something of a goofball, but how could I ever resent a kid who had shown such wonderfully perceptive taste in music?

That Won't Do You Any Good

Mom on a Horse

Imagine this: Two thugs have just broken into my house, slammed me into a chair and put a gun to my head. They tell me they have a little wager for me, if I care to participate.

"Let's make a bet," says one of the heavy breathers. "If we can find a photo of your mother riding a horse we get to pull the trigger. If we can't, you get ten dollars. Wanna play?"

It's at this point that I laugh in their dim-witted faces. Of *course* I want to play. Who couldn't use an extra ten bucks? And my mother on a horse? And I laugh again. And then I'm dead.

I found it today when I was going through the box of old photos I had brought back after emptying my parents' house. It was a picture of Dad riding on a horse. Next to him, somewhat further back actually, was a woman, also riding a horse. Could that be Mom? And if it is, how is that even possible?

The photo was taken during a vacation to Pennsylvania that my parents took in the early 1970's. They were already in their mid-forties by this time, but seeing Dad atop a horse was no surprise. He had always been athletic, and led an active life nearly right up until the day he died. In the box I had found pictures of him hunting, fishing, swimming, as well as playing baseball and football. And so, though I had never known him to ride a horse, I wasn't particularly surprised to see that he had.

Mom, as far as I knew, had never done anything more athletic than using all seven tiles in a game of Scrabble. Growing up we had a built-in pool in our backyard, and I still remember the only two times that my mom went in it, and one of those times was because my little brother had pushed her in.

It was difficult to positively identify Mom in the photo, and so I did a little detective work. I looked at several of the other shots from that same trip and there it was: In two other pictures Mom was wearing the exact jacket as the woman on the horse. Yes, that woman riding on the horse, and looking quite comfortable doing it, was indeed my very own mother.

Only four years after the photo was taken I myself, at the age of twenty-two, would ride a horse for the first, and no doubt last, time in my life. And here was my mom, at almost exactly twice that age, proudly clip-clopping down the trail like some kind of suburban Dale Evans. It makes me wonder what else I never knew about my mother. I'm almost afraid to look at the rest of the photos.

Made in United States
North Haven, CT
26 February 2023